George Alfred Townsend

The Swamp Outlaws

George Alfred Townsend

The Swamp Outlaws

ISBN/EAN: 9783337336820

Printed in Europe, USA, Canada, Australia, Japan

Cover: Foto ©Suzi / pixelio.de

More available books at **www.hansebooks.com**

THE SWAMP OUTLAWS:

OR,

THE NORTH CAROLINA BANDITS.

BEING A COMPLETE HISTORY OF

THE MODERN ROB ROYS AND ROBIN HOODS.

NEW-YORK:
ROBERT M. DE WITT, PUBLISHER,
NO. 33 ROSE STREET,
(Between Duane and Frankfort Streets)

INTRODUCTION.

The homely old adage that there is nothing "new under the sun" is constantly verified by actual facts occuring every day. The accounts handed down by tradition of "the bold archer Robin Hood" keeping whole counties on the alert, and disputing the right to kill fat bucks in the royal forest with the boldest barons, have seemed almost too daring for belief, yet here we have—in this enlightened period of the world's history—a whole State of the most powerful and most enlightened nation of the earth successfully defied by a band of less than a dozen Outlaws. Individual hunters essay to track and capture them, and their bones bleach in the forest paths for their temerity, troops—regular and irregular—attempt their subjugation, and are ingloriously repelled by these dauntles, law-defying Bandits.

Not only are they secure in their swampy retreats. They boldly make raids into the neighboring country, and release prisoners from the constituted authorities. They fearlessly enter towns and deliberately carry off the municipal archives and county treasures—removing by main force immense Herring safes, whose strength baffled violence and whose ingeniously-constructed locks no skill could open.

The most fertile brain never conjured up such deeds of courage, cruelty and skillful military stratagem as have marked the career of these undaunted men, in whose veins the blood of the Indian and Negro is strangely commingled. Indeed, it seems as if the white *Frankenstein* by his crimes has raised a fearful monster that will not down at the bidding of his affrighted master.

Strange, unlikely and almost incredible as the deeds may appear which crimson the sluggish swamp streams of the Old North State, and which are graphically narrated in the following pages, they may be relied on as perfectly authentic. They are collected from the columns of the *New York Herald*. It seems almost superfluous, at this late day, to say anything in praise of the wonderful resources and world-reaching enterprises of this great journal. At a time when the proprietor of the Herald is supporting a corps of brave men in the dense tropical forests of Africa, seeking to reach and save *Livingstone* (a task, by the way, that his own government has shrank from); when his correspondents are interviewing Bismarck and comparing notes with Gladstone—he finds time and means to send an intelligent correspondent right into the heart of the country where the red bowie-knife and death-dealing rifles of the Swamp Outlaws are carrying dismay and terror into the hearts of men, women and children. Indeed, there appears to be nothing too small for its microscopic or too large for its telescopic vision. A Baxter street fight or a Sedan conflict alike find in the ubiqitous columns of the New York Herald "a local habitation and a name,"

THE SWAMP OUTLAWS.

Among the Lowerys, the Outlaw Terrors of North Carolina—Tuscarora, Senegal and Caucasian Blood Mingling in Their Veins—History of their Campaign—A Bloody Nine Years' Record—Sixteen Murders,—Three Hundred Robberies, and Not a Man Lost to the Band—Hopeless Condition of Affairs—The Old North State Dismayed and Baffled—Graphic Pen Picture of Henry Berry Lowery, the Outlaw Chief—Portraits of "Boss" Strong, Steve Lowery, Andrew Strong and Tom Lowery.

SHOE HEEL, N. C., Feb. 27, 1872. The bandit of North Carolina, Henry Berry Lowery, standing in perfect disdain of the authorities of the State, as well as of the federal troops, it was deemed necessary to send a HERALD correspondent to study the situation.

TO THE SEAT OF WAR.

I left Washington City Thursday night and reported myself next day at noon in the office of Governor Walker of Virginia.

The handsomest man in the South was seated at the table, signing bills, in the old Confederate Supreme Court room. His beautiful, grayish black mustache, healthy gray hair, clear skin and smiling expression, every inch a lord lieutenant in the oldest of our shires, grew soberer as he said:—

"Lowery? Why a captain of the Virginia militia applied to me yesterday to obtain permission for himself and forty men to hunt that fellow in the swamps of North Carolina. Lowery must be a good deal of a character."

As I looked over the files of the Richmond newspapers, and their intimate exchanges of the tobacco, rice and tar region, I found the question of the day to be—Lowery. He was at once the Nat Turner, the Osceola, and the Rob Roy MacGregor of the South. With mingled ardor and anxiety, desire and trepidation, I pushed on by the Weldon road to Wilmington, the largest town of the State, where Lowery had once been confined in prison. There was there but a single question—Lowery. The Wilmington papers called the Robeson county people cowards for not cleaning him out. The Robeson county paper hurled back the insinuation, but hurled nothing else at Lowery. The State government got its share of the blame, and the State Adjutant General replied in a card that the militia and volunteers had no pluck on the occasion when he had tried them. Five men had mastered a Commonwealth.

THE SCARE ON THE ROAD.

An instance of the deep sense of apprehension created by these bandits in all southeastern Carolina is afforded by a dream which Colonel W. H. Barnard, editor of the Wilmington *Star*, related to me. The Colonel's paper is eighty miles from the scene of outlawry:

"I dreamed the other night," said he, "that I was riding up the Rutherford Railroad, and came to Moss Neck station, where the outlaws frequently ap-

[ix.]

pear. I thought a yellow fellow, Indian-looking, came to the car door and said, 'Everybody can pass but Barnard! I want him!' This was Henry Berry Lowery. Then I dreamed they took me into some kind of torture place, and poked guns at me and tantalized me."

The newspapers were, however, making political capital out of the Lowery gang, instead of calling upon an honorable and united State sentiment to suppress the scandal. The democratic papers cried, "Black Ku Klux!" and the republican papers retorted by asking where was the valor of the white Ku Klux, who could flog a thousand peaceful men, but dared not meet five outlaws in arms.

"The democrats," said one Robeson county man, in my room, "as soon as they upset the republicans in Robeson county started to annihilate Scuffle-town and its vote by terror. They have been beaten in it. That chap Lowery has made them a laughing stock. He ought to be killed, but they skulk out of his reach."

CRIME WITHOUT A COMPASS.

Mayor Martin, of Wilmington, President of the Rutherford Railway, which passes through Scuffle-town and the land of the outlaws, relates an incident, pitiful at least to Northern ears, of the ignorance of these robbers, and the hopeless fight they are making within the limits of all that is available to them. Adjutant General Gorham, who directed the late ignominious campaign against the Lowery band—where, by current reports, the main victories gained were over the mulatto women, the soldiery driving the husbands forth to insult and debauch their wives—said that Henry Berry Lowery, when asked to withdraw from the State, replied:—

"Robeson county is the only land I know. I can hardly read, and do not know where to go if I leave these woods and swamps, where I was raised. If I can get safe conduct and pardon I will go anywhere. I will join the United States Army and fight the Indians. But these people will not let me leave alive, and I do not mean to enter any jail again. I will never give up my gun."

Mayor Martin's solution for the difficulty is for the United States to declare martial law over the whole Congressional district in which Robeson county stands, and make a systematic search with regular troops for these outlaws. He says that when they first took to their excursions they were comparitively sober, but of late have taken to drinking, and about four weeks ago they all, except their leader, got drunk at Ed. Smith's store, Moss Neck, and lay there all night! "Whiskey," said Mayor Martin, "will reduce them in time; but they are very careful whose liquor they drink in these days. Henry Berry Lowery left his flask hanging on a fence a few weeks ago, and when he returned to get it he made everybody at the station drink with him."

TO LUMBERTON.

Early in the morning, Monday, February 26, I took the train for Lumberton, and from the forward car to the tail the freight was Lowery. In the second class carriage, escorted by two sheriffs, MacMillan and Brown, of Robeson county, was Pop Oxendine—the previous said to be his literal name—brother of Henderson Oxendine, the only one of the outlaws who was ever brought to trial and hanged. He was chained to a regular army soldier, who had recently murdered a negro at Scuffletown, and he was a remarkable looking mulatto, with a yellowish olive skin, good features, and a handsome, appealing, unreliable, uninterpretable pair of black eyes. So good looking a mulatto man, with such a complexion, I had not seen. Like the rest, he had the Tuscarora Indian blood in him, with the duplicity of the mixed races where the white blood predominates. He was ironed fast to the seat and looked at me with a look inquisitive, pitiful, evasive and ingenuous by turns. If I should describe the man by the words nearest my idea I should call him a negro-Indian gypsy.

The passengers were apprehensive and inquisitive together, wanting to know all about Lowery and dreading to encounter him. The fullest, and often very intelligent, explanations were made to me, and every facility was tendered to assist me to form accurate conclusions as to the characters in the band.

Colonel S. L. Fremont, General Superintendent of the Rutherford Railway, will permit no passenger carrying arms for the purpose of shooting Lowery to ride on his trains, as he fears that such permission will endanger the safety of the railway. Lowery could toss a train off almost any day, but he seems to hold a superstitious respect for the United States mails.

A few months ago a man by the name of Marsden announced that he meant to travel up and down the road as a detective and kill Lowery on sight. To put him to the test Lowery and all the band appeared with cocked shotguns at Moss Neck station, and stood at a respectable, yet furtive, "present arms," while the braggart, for such he was, crawled under the car seat. Lowery offered $100 reward to anybody who would tell him whether Marden or Marsden was on the train, as he meant to follow the fellow up the road but he would not cross the platform himself.

The conductors and engineers say that there is perfect safety on the trains, although none know when the outlaw leader may take offence against the company or its officers.

LUMBERTON IN COURT WEEK.

The Rutherford Railway traverses the counties of the southern tier of North Carolina, passing few towns of the magnitude, but built generally through the pitch pine woods, whose white boles, stripped a few feet from the ground and notched to provoke the flow of the sap and to catch it, resemble the interminable tombstones of a woodland burial ground. Swamps intersect the woods, and the resinous-looking waters of many creeks and canals alternate with deserted rice fields, the skeletons of old turpentine distilleries, the stubble of ragged cotton plantations, some occasional weather-blackened shanties, and now and then a sawmill or a pile of newly hewn timber.

Flat, humid, almost uninhabited, is the traveller's first impression of the country. But there is a speck of light and life at Abbottsville, the home of ex-United States Senator Abbott, who has built up the "Cape Fear Building Company," to supply ready made houses to the people of his adopted State, and whose private residence, of yellow frame, is next to the large mill and branch railway of the enterprise.

After five hours ride we came to the weather-blackened, unpainted town of Lumberton, on the flowing Lumber River, a branch of the Pedee.

Lumberton is the seat of Robeson county, the stamping ground of Lowery's band. With one exception—and that disputable as the act of the band—no murder has been committed by the Lowerys beyond the lines of this county. It contains, by the census of 1870, 3,042 men above the age of twenty-one.

By the census of 1850, the last preceeding census available at this point of view, it contained 639 whites unable to read, and had at that time 1,171 free negroes, or more than even the populous county in which Wilmington stands, and quintuple the free negroes population of the adjacent counties.

Scuffletown a few miles distant from Lumberton was one of the largest free negro settlements in the United States before the war against slavery, and it was besides, an almost immemorial free negro settlement.

This being Court week, the town of Lumberton was full of Scuffletowners, and I saw and talked with Sinclair Lowery, elder brother of the outlaws, and also with "Dick" Oxendine, who married the only sister of Henry Berry Lowery, and who keeps a barroom in the Court House village.

Besides, I visited the scene of the latest exploits of the Lowerys, the capture of the most valuable safe in the town, as well as the county official safe, which they contemptuously rejected on the road.

I also visited the jail where Henderson Oxendine's gallows stood, and the court room, where a noisy crier made proclamation from the open window, and the garrulous Judge Clarke was delivering a charge upon the enormities of these banditti, crying meantime into his pocket handkerchief.

Besides, I talked with a great number of the leading citizens, who, to a man, were of Scotch descent, and at noon next day, resuming the train, I visited Scuffletown and slept with courteous entertainers at Shoe Heel, in the heart of the pine forest.

The incidents of these excursions will appear hereafter.

Let me now address myself to describing the outlaws.

DESCRIPTION OF THE OUTLAWS.

HENRY BERRY LOWERY.

Henry Berry Lowery, the leader of the most formidable band of outlaws, considering the smallness of its numbers, that has been known in this country, is of mixed Tuscarora, mulatto and white blood, twenty-six years of age, five feet nine inches high and weighing about 150 pounds.

He has straight black hair, like an Indian: a dark goatee, and a beard graceful in shape, but too thin to look very black. His face slopes from the cheek bones to the tip of his goatee, so as to give him the Southern American contour of physiognomy; but it is lighted with eyes of a different color—eyes of a grayish hazel—at times appearing light blue, with a drop of brown in them, but in agitation dilating, darkening, and, although never quite losing the appearance of a smile, yet in action it is a smile of devilish nature.

His forehead is good and his face and expression refined—remarkably so, considering his mixed race, want of education and long career of lawlessness.

A scar of crescent shape and black color lies in the skin below his left eye, said to have been made by an iron pot falling upon him when a child.

His voice is sweet and pleasant, and in his manner there is nothing self-important or swaggering. He is not talkative, listens quietly, and searches out whoever is speaking to him like a man illiterate in all books save the two great books of nature, and human nature above all.

MRS. HENRY LOWERY

The color of the skin is of a whitish yellow sort, with an admixture of copper—such a skin as, for the nature of its components, is in color indescribable, there being no negro blood in it except that of a far remote generation of mulatto, and the Indian still apparent.

It is enough to say of this skin that it seems to suffer little change by heat or cold, exposure or sickness, good houseing or wild weather.

The very relatives of white men killed by Henry Berry Lowery admitted to me that "He is one of the handsomest mulattoes you ever saw."

LOWERY PHYSICALLY.

To match this face the outlaw's body is of mixed strength and beauty.

It is well knit, wiry, straight in the shoulders and limbs, without a physical flaw in it, and as one said to me who had known him well since childhood, "He is like a trap ball, elastic all over."

He has feet which would be noticeable anywhere, pointed and with arching instep, so that he can wear a very shapely boot, and his extremities, like his features indicate nothing of the negro. A good chest, long bones, suppleness, proportion, make his walk and form pleasing to see.

He is negligent about his dress, but his clothes become him and never disparage him.

People have told me that he wore fine clothes; but, when questioned to the point of re-examination, admitted that he had nothing on but a woolen blouse and trousers and a black wide-brimmed, stiff woolen hat.

HIS ARMS.

To see this trim youth as he appears whenever seen on the highroads or the piney forest bypath, or as often at the railway stations of Moss Neck, Eureka, Bule's Store, or Red Banks, is to see young Mars bearing about an arsenal.

His equipment might appear preposterous if we do not consider, the peculiar circumstances of his warfare—outlawed by the state of North Carolina, without a reliable base of supplies, and compelled to carry arms and charges in them enough to encounter a large body of men or stand a long campaign.

A belt around his waist accommodates five six-barrelled revolvers—long shooters.

From this belt a shoulder strap passes up and supports behind, slinging fashion, a Spencer rifle, which carries eight cartridges, and it is now generally alleged that he has replaced this with a Henry rifle, carrying double the former number of cartridges, while, successively, man after man of the band, by some mysterious agency, becomes possessed of a Spencer rifle. In addition to these forty or forty-eight charges Lowery carries a long-bladed knife and a large flask of whiskey—the latter because he fears to be poisoned by promiscuous neighborhood drinking.

He can run like a deer, swim, stand weeks of exposure in the swamps and o rest, walk day and night, and take sleep by little snatches which, in a few days, would tire out white or negro.

Although a tippler, he was never known to be drunk—a fact not to be justly asserted by his confederates.

Brought suddenly at bay he is observed to wear that light, fiendish, enjoying smile, which shows a nature at its depths savage, predatory and fond of blood. The war he has waged for the past nine years, within a region of twelve or fifteen miles square, against county, State, Confederate and United States authorities, alternately or unitedly is justification for the terror apparent in the faces of all the white people within those limits.

Lowery's band gives more concern to the Carolinas than did Carleton's Legion ninety years ago.

LOWERY AS A BRIGAND LEADER.

"What is the meaning of this?" said I to "Parson" Sinclair—the fighting parson of Lumberton—"How can this fellow, with a handful of boys and illiterate men, put to flight a society only recently used to warfare and full of accomplished soldiers? Explain it."

"Lowery," answered Sinclair, "is really one of those remarkable executive spirits that arises now and then in a raw community, without advantages other than nature gave him. He has passions, but no weaknesses, and his eye is on every point at once. He has impressed that whole negro society with his power and influence. They fear and admire him. He asserts his superiority over all these whites just as well. No man who stands face to face with him can resist his quiet will, and assurance and his searching eye. Without fear, without hope, defying society, he is the only man we have any knowledge of down here who can play his part.

Upon my word, I believe if he had lived ages ago he would have been a William the Conqueror. He reminds me of nobody but Rob Roy."

HIS BLOOD AND INCLINATIONS.

The three natures of white, Indian and negro are, however, seen at intervals to come forward in this outlaw's nature.

The negro trace is in his love of rude music.

He is a banjo player, and when the periodical hunt for him is done he repairs to some one of the huts in Scuffletown and plays to the dancing of the mulatto girls and his companions by the hour, his belt of arms unslung and thrown at his feet, the peaceable part of the audience taking part with mixed wonder delight and apprehension. Several times this banjo has nearly betrayed him to his pursuers.

Sheriff MacMillan described himself and posse once lying out all night in the swamp and timber around Lowery's cabin to wait for him to come forth at daylight.

"And," said he, "that banjo was just everlastingly thrumming, and we could hear the laughter and Juba-beating nearly the whole night long."

THE MULATTO SARDANAPALUS.

The licentiousness of Lowery is sufficient to be noticeable, but while it never engages him to the exclusion of vigilance and activity, it also shows what may be traced in some degree to his Indian nature—the using of women as an auxiliary to war and plunder.

He has debauched a number of his prisoners with the mulatto girls of Scuffletown, and the charms of these yellow-tinted syrens broke up the *morale* of the late campaign in force against the outlaws, while, as some allege, the discovery of the Detective Sanders' plan to capture Lowery was made by a girl in Lowery's interest with whom Sanders spent his time.

Lowery has said, and laughed over it, that he devised at a critical point in a truce between the contending parties that a bevy of the prettiest and frailest beauties in Scuffletown should come up and be introduced to one of the officers high in command.

After that the Marc Antony in question laid down his sword, and gave practical evidence that the hostility of races is not so great as the slavery statesmen alleged.

The indifference of the Indian to the loan of his squaws finds some parallel in Lowery's tactics.

He himself is the Don Juan of Scuffletown; but he sleeps on his arms, and will go into the swamps for weeks without repining. Women have been employed to give him up; but they either repent or he discovers their purpose by intuitive sagacity.

THE OUTLAW'S WIFE.

The white society around him gave Henry Berry Lowery a lesson in self-schooling and sacrifice so far as women were concerned.

After the murders of Barnes and Harris — offences which, some think, ought to have been included in the proclamation of oblivion for offences committed by both sides before the close of the war—Lowery stood up by the side of Rhody Strong, the most beautiful mulatto of Scuffletown, to be married.

Aware of the engagement and the occasion, the Sheriff's posse, with cruel deliberation, surrounded the house till the ceremony was over, and then rushed in and took the outlawed husband from the side of his wife.

He was removed to Lumberton jail, and then sent still further away to Columbus county jail; but he broke through the bars, escaped to the woods with the irons on his wrists, and made his way to his bride. They have three children, the fruit of their stolen and rudely interrupted interviews.

A GLIMPSE AT MADAME LOWERY.

As I rode down on the train from Shoe Heel to Lumberton, on the 28th of February, the conductor, Colonel Morrison, came to me and said:—" if you want to see Henry Berry Lowery's wife you can find her in the forward second-class car."

She had taken the train at Red Banks for Moss Neck—points between which the whole band of outlaws frequently ride on the freight trains—and at the latter notable station I saw her descend with her baby and walk off down the road in the woods and stop there among the tall pitch pines, as if waiting for somebody. The baby—the last heir of outlawry—began to cry as she left the train, and she said, mother-fashion: "No, no, no, I wouldn't cry, when I had been so good all day!"

This woman is the sister of two of the five remaining outlaws and wife of the third.

The whites call her satirically, "the queen of Scuffletown;" but she appeared to be a meek, pretty-eyed rather shrinking girl, of a very light color, poorly dressed.

She wore many brass rings, with cheap rep stones in them, on her small hands, and a dark green plaid dress of muslin delaine, which just revealed her new black morocco "store" shoes. A yellowish muslin or calico hood, with a long cape, covered her head, and there was nothing beside that I remember except a shawl of bright colors, much worn.

It was sad enough and prosaic enough to see this small woman with her baby in her arms, carrying it along, while the husband and father, covered with the blood of fifteen murders, roamed the woods and swamps like a Seminole.

Rhody Lowery is said not to be a constant wife, but to follow the current example of Scuffletown. Other persons, the negroes notably, deny this.

A more persevering newspaper correspondent might settle the issue.

LOWERY AS A TERRORIZER.

Mr. Hayes, a republican, of Shoe Heel, whose knowledge of the Scuffletown settlement is very good and whose practical Northern mind is not likely to be deceived, told me that Lowery, among his numerous warnings served upon people, stopped one white man on the road and said, "You are taking advantage of my circumstances and absence to be familiar with my family. Now, you better pack up and get out of this county."

The man lost no time in doing as requested; for Henry Berry Lowery generally warns before he kills. In the matter of honesty in the observance of a promise or a treaty the people most robbed and outraged by this bandit acknowledge his Indian scrupulousness. "Mr. MacNair," he said to one of his white neighbors, whom he had robbed twenty times, "I want you to gear up and go to Lumberton, where they have put my wife in jail for no crime but because she is my wife; that ain't her fault, and they can't make it so. You people won't let me work to get my living, and I have got to take it from you; but, God knows, she'd like to see me make my own bread. You go to Lumberton and tell the Sheriff and County Commissioners that if they don't let her out of that jail I'll retaliate on the white women of Burnt Swamp Township. Some of them shall come to the swamp with me if she is kept in the jail, because they can't get me."

LOWERY AS A TRUCE MAKER.

Lowery then named a point on the road where he would meet MacNair, and he met him instead three miles nearer to Lumberton. The feeling of terror in the county may be understood when, without more delay, Rhody Lowery was set free.

While in the region several persons urged me to go out and talk to Lowery Sheriff MacMillan and Mr. Brown, the son-in-law of the murdered Sheriff King —strange as it may appear for county officers, and I mention it to show the superstition inspired by this brigand— offered to obtain an interview for me with the whole gang by sending out some member of the Lowery family to negotiate. My faith was not equal to theirs, and I declined.

"Do you suppose that fellow would give me a talk?" I said to Calvin Black a merchant of Shoe Heel.

"Yes, if he could be made to understand that your intentions were pacific. The large reward now out for him, amounting, for himself and party, to about forty-five thousand dollars, taken dead or alive, makes him apprehensive of assassination. But if he were to promise not to injure you, you could go anywhere to see him with perfect impunity." This was general testimony.

Rev. Mr. MacDiermid, editor of the *Robesonian*, the county organ, who does his duty by unintimidated denunciation of this outlaw, said:—"Henry Berry Lowery has sent me word that I had better be cautious how I write about him, but I believe that I could go to see him to-day, for he appreciates his consequence in the *role* he has assumed." I noticed, however, that nobody did go to see him, and I followed that high and general example.

PRICE OF LOWERY'S HEAD.

Since Jefferson Davis' flight and the reward put upon his head there has been no American criminal—probably none previously in all the history of the country for offences at common law—who has been dignified with the amount of money offered for Lowery's overtaking.

If it should appear in the North this sketch is too strong, I point to this reward and to the fact that this outlaw has already made a personal and bloody campaign against society longer than the whole revolutionary war.

Osceola, or Powel (who was an immediate mixture of Indian and negro blood, and who fought over a larger region), gave out in a much shorter space of resistance.

HIS CHIVALRY.

Two things are to be chronicled in this man's favor, and I make them on the universal testimony of everybody in this region.

He has never committed arson or rape or offered to insult females. While entering private houses nearly every day his worst act is to drive the family into some one apartment and bar them there while the house is cooly and leisurely ransacked.

A few weeks ago an aged lady, Mrs. MacNeil and her daughter, were shot with duck shot by somebody taking the name of Lowery's band, doubtless the party accused; but the wounding of the woman was not foreseen by the brigands, and they fired at old MacNeil, whose family of sons and son-in-law had become particularly offensive to them.

MacNeil told me the circumstances as follows:—He had been repeatedly robbed, his son-in-law Taylor killed, his sons ordered to leave the country, and now almost entirely alone, he was compelled to do a good deal of his own watching and to wait upon himself.

Standing by his smokehouse one moonlight night he saw two men enter the yard and one of them walked straight up to the smokehouse door and began to pry it open. Partly concealed in the shadow of the fence, MacNeil cried—

"Who is that?"

No answer.

He repeated the interrogation and the reply was—

"What in the hell is that your business?"

The Scotch blood of the old man mounted to his face, notwithstanding his long and not wholly undeserved misfortunes, and he went into his dwelling for his gun. His wife and his daughter besought him not to venture out, and, on his refusal, followed him to the door. He called again:—

"Who's that at my smokehouse?"

The answer was:—

"Lowery's band, God damn you." And in a minute a charge of buckshot poured in at the door, putting, as MacNeil said, sixteen buckshot in a place no bigger than his hat from the spot where he was expected to have been, and striking his wife in the thigh, riddling her dress, and hitting his daughter in the shoulder and breast, so that the shot came out of her back. Both women will recover, although sorely wounded.

The cause of this long persecution of MacNeil I will give in another letter.

RUMORS AND INCIDENTS.

Colonel Wischart, an old Confederate officer and a dauntless man, living near Moss Neck, has shot at Lowery several times, but always missed him, and once surrounded with a posse the outlaw's cabin, but he got off so mysteriously that they allege to this day that he had an underground passage.

Lowery is said to whip his wife sometimes and to have threatened also to shoot her, on the occasions of her reproving his long absences. Some time ago she came, according to rumor, to a store at Lumberton and remarked:—

"Berry put his gun in my face to-day and said he meant to kill me, and I told him to fire it off—not to stop for me."

The negroes charge that these stories are without foundation, and Deputy Sheriff Brown admitted to me:—

. "Lowery will never leave this country alive."

"Why?"

"Because he loves his wife and will not leave her whereabouts."

I give some further rumors for what they are worth:—

Henry B. Lowery is not a good shot except at close quarters—so says Boss Strong. The Boss remarked at Moss Neck one day:—

"Henry is nothing much with that Spencer rifle, nor his shotgun, neither; but Steve Lowery can shoot the tail off a coon."

Some of the Scuffletown negroes say differently, and give marvellous instances of the accuracy of eye and nerve of both Henry Berry and the majority of the gang. He certainly generally kills when he does shoot. Here is an instance of his coolness. A Mr. McRae who lives on the limits of Robeson county removed from the immediate country of the bandits, got off with other passengers at Moss Neck a few weeks ago, and said aloud familiarly—

"Where does this rascal, Lowery,

keep himself? I'd like to see the villain."

A whitish negro, standing near by, unarmed, said, coolly—

"Well, sir, if you'll step this way I'll show him to you."

This was Tom Lowery. The astonished pasenger was put in a moment in the presence of a sombre-looking mulatto fellow with straight hair, whose body was girt all round with pistols, and who carried two guns besides.

"This is Henry Berry Lowery," said the other outlaw.

"Yes," said Henry, "and we always ask our friends to take a drink with us."

The passenger saw the significant bland look on both the half-breed faces, and he said, with all available assurance:—

"I'll take the drink if you'll let me pay for it."

"Oh, yes, we always expect our friends to treat us."

PICTURE OF "SWARTHY INDIAN STEVE."

The brigand of the Lowery gang, in appearance, is Steve, whose carriage is that of a New York rough, and whose thick, black, straight hair, thin, black moustache, goatee and very lowering countenance, set with blackish hazel eyes, give him the character his deeds bear out of a robber and murderer of the Murrel stamp.

He is the most perfect Indian of the party, superadded to the vagabond. He is five feet nine inches high, thick set, round shouldered, heavy and of powerful strength, with long arms, a heavy mouth, and that brusque, aggressive, impudent manner, which befits the highwayman stopping his man.

Steve Lowery required no great provocation to take to the swamps and prowl around the country by day and night.

He is mentioned third on the list in the Governor's proclamation, figuring there at $500, or half the price of Henry Berry Lowry's head; is the oldest of the gang, said to be thirty-one, and his imperious temper, insatiable love of robbery and insubordination to his younger brother, the leader, once involved him in a quarrel, where he was shot in the leg.

Steve has the worst countenance of any man in the gang. His swarthy, dark brown complexion, thin visage and quick speech make him feared by any unlucky enemy who may fall into the hands of the outlaws.

When Landers, the detective, was condemned to death and Tom Lowery slunk away, unwilling to see blood, Steve Lowery raised his gun and filled the unfortunate prisoner with a charge of buckshot. Steve has been concerned in nearly every robbery and shooting, perhaps every one, committed by this party.

SKETCH OF BOSS STRONG.

The youngest of the gang and the most trusted and inseparable companion of Henry Berry Lowery is his boy brother-in-law, Boss Strong, aged no more than twenty. The Strongs are said to have been derived from a white man of that name, who came from Western Carolina to Scuffletown and took up with one of the Lowery women. In this generation they are legitimate. Boss Strong is nearly white; his dark, short cut hair has a reddish tinge and is slightly curling; a thick down appears on his lip and temples, but otherwise he is beardless; he has that dull, blueish eye frequently seen among the Scuffle-. tonians, and is taciturn.

In repose his countenance is mild and pleasing; but the demon is always near at hand when Henry Berry Lowery desires it to appear, and then the heavy black eye-brows of the boy, which nearly meet over the bridge of his nose, give him a dogged, determined look, which many a man has seen to his cost. Boss Strong is plastic material in the hands of his brother-in-law, and next to that leader is commonly regarded as the worst of the party.

He is so distinguished in all the offers of rewards. Being the least capable and experienced of the party, he is therefore most dangerous in other hands, and it is a revolting instance of the extremes of good and ill to see the fidelity of Boss Strong to Henry Berry Lowery up to the consummation of repeated murders with the coolest military obedience.

His hands are dyed deep in the blood of old and young. Boss Strong is about five feet ten, thick set, with a full face, and he handles his arms with skill and has the courage of a bull pup.

When John Taylor's brains were blown out by Henry Berry, Boss rushed upon the bank and aimed at young MacNeil and wounded him with the wad of a charge of buckshot intended to slay him.

The people of Robeson county and the military authorities have long ago given up all prospect of seducing either of these murderers to betray each other.

Boss Strong has never been considered as within that possibility. He, like the leading outlaw, has generally killed his man at close quarters—seldom at more than from four to ten yards.

ANDREW STRONG DELINEATED.

Andrew Strong, elder brother of Boss, is very nearly the same age with Henry Berry Lowery. He is more than six feet high, tall and slim, and nearly perfectly white; his thin beard is of a reddish tinge, and he has dark, straight hair.

This fellow is the Oily Gammon of the party, without that higher order of cunning which with Henry Berry Lowery amounts to prescience and strategy; but his eye can wear a look of meek, reproachful injury, and his tongue is soft and treacherous.

He was at one time in Court, and when the indictment of his crimes was read he looked out of his great, soft eyes as if ready to weep at such unjust imputations. Andrew Strong married the daughter of Henry Sampson, another of the Indian mulattoes, and has two children.

He is a cowardly cutthroat, and will steal a pocketbook on the high road.

In the way of killing people he is similarly perfidious, and the honey will drop from his tongue almost into the wound he inflicts. Loving to see fear and pain, a professor of deceit, plausible, uncertain, uneasy, deadly, this meanest of the band yet has consequence in it.

TOM LOWERY, THE JAIL BIRD.

Tom Lowery has a long, straight Caucasian nose, a good forehead of more than average height, sloping but heavy jaws, very scrubby, black beard about the chin, coming out short, stiff and sparse, and straight, black hair.

He would be called cadaverous if he were white, but in his eye there are the hazel lights (darting and restless, and readily burning up to a large glow) of the Indian gypsy. Perhaps the solution of the white race, which blended originally with the Tuscaroras—a subject on which the learned Judge Leech, of Lumberton, has spent much inquiry—might be solved by the gypsy suggestion. The Judge mentioned Portuguese (a truly piratical race since the days of Tolsnois), Spanish and several other races to

VIEW OF THE PRINCIPAL STREET IN SCUFFLETOWN.

account for the blood which others attributed in the Lowerys to negro infusion. Might it have been "Rommany?" The English gypsy has been in North America a hundred years.

Tom Lowery is a thieving sneak, capable of murder, but sickened by blood, and the oldest member of the Lowery gang.

He is thirty-five years of age, has a broad-shouldered, active, strong body, and is five feet nine inches high.

The eye of this man is a study—blueish gray, furtive, and dancing around, but when the observer's eye drops away he sends a heathenish shaft of light straight out from the thieving nature of the fellow, which seems to seize all the situation.

He is equally alert in slipping jail and evading capture, and some time ago he got off from the military, peppered all over the back with shot and with his shirt full of blood.

THE RETIRED PSEUDO OR DISABLED BANDITS.

The above five men constitute, at present, the bandits and outlaws of North Carolina. Together they make an active and formidable, and also a wicked crowd; and, officered by a man of remarkable ability and powers, they present an anomalous picture in the heart of modern society.

I append sketches of the other and former members of the band, and now in the foreground:—

GEORGE APPLEWHITE

George Applewhite is a regular negro, of a surly, determined look, with thick features, woolly hair, large protuberances above the eyebrows, big jaws and cheek bones and a black eye.

He is a picture of a slave at bay. Mrs. Stowe might have drawn "Dred" from him.

He is supposed either to be dead, hidden away, wounded, or to have abandoned the country, as he has not been seen or heard of for several months.

When last heard from he was faint from loss of blood, and had received wounds in the breast from some soldiery.

He married into the Oxendine family, and was present at the murder of Sheriff King and elsewhere, and is therefore included in the list of outlaws and a reward put upon his head.

JOHN DIAL, THE STATE'S EVIDENCE.

John Dial, who lies in the jail of Columbus county, at Whitesville, as Calvin Lowery does in the jail of New Hanover county, at Wilmington, is a light mulatto, with a vagrant, fierce look, aggravated by a wart or fleshy protuberance of some sort on the side of his nose, directly beside the left eye, which wart is as large as a marble.

Dial was as bad as any of the gang, but not bold, and he prefers the repose of the jail to wading the swamps with Henry Lowery.

He says that George Applewhite shot Sheriff King, while the rest of the band charge that Dial himself precipitately drew his pistol and killed that hale old Carolinian.

SHOEMAKER JOHN.

"Shoemaker John," who at one time had dealings with Henry Berry Lowery's party, but has been sent to the Penitentiary, is an oval-faced negro, good for stealing, but with little stomach for blood-letting. The Lowerys repudiate him altogether.

THE ONE MAN HANGED

Henderson Oxendine, hanged at Lumberton some time ago, was a thick-set but trim light mulatto, with straight hair and a stoical face. He died without more than a sigh.

I visited Calvin Oxendine in the Wilmington jail, whence nearly the whole band escaped, he refusing or being afraid to go.

CALVIN OXENDINE.

The Wilmington jail is an oblong brick structure, to the front of which is affixed the jailor's residence of a plaster imitation of sandstone crowned with battlements.

The jail is small in size, as big as a country meeting-house, and the rear part and body of it descends below the street level into a sunken lot, which is enclosed by a brick wall capped with nails and broken glass.

From the upper tier of jail windows to the ground, is about thirty feet, and the walls is twelve feet high. A fierce dog goes at large in the jail yard.

Our worthies occupied one of the rear corner cells in the upper tier of this jail for six months, and they took out the bricks at the side of the edifice, making a small hole, still in outlines distinctly visible though re-enclosed, and let themselves down with their blankets.

The dog made no alarm, if, as is doubtful, he was at liberty that night, and the neighboring vacant lots gave easy means of escape to our bandit desperadoes.

The jail is, like most county jails in the South, a piece of dilapidation without, and of bad construction within, and other holes in the rear attest how other prisoners made their riddance.

One of these holes, at the present writing, has not been bricked up, although some time has elapsed since the inmates cut it.

THE BANDIT IN JAIL.

I visited this jail with the courteous City Marshal of Wilmington, W. P. Canaday, first entering a livery stable adjacent, through the open chinks of which tools were, probably, handed to the prisoners within, the level being nearly the same and the walls only twenty feet apart.

The jail, in the interior, was of an inhuman architecture, the cells being enclosed by a corridor, which debarred them from light and gave only ventillation by shafts above.

The grated doors admitted very little light through their narrow chinks, and murderer or mere peace-breaker shared a common fate in them, lying almost in darkness.

A prison without security for the evil ought to afford some compensation for the merely erring, suspected or unfortunate.

This jail, while clean enough, is a relic of the Middle Ages.

If you take from a man liberty give him at least light! One of the iron doors was laboriously unlocked by the negro jailor, and shaking himself from the long vision of darkness, Calvin Oxendine, an indicted murderer of Sheriff King, walked out into the corridor.

Here was a situation for John Calvin, the Richelieu of the Huguenots! That name, crossing from France to Scotland and passing into the family nomenclature of Gael and Lowlander, had made the passage of the ocean with the immigrants into Carolina, and these mixed mulattoes and Indians had inherited it from their Scotch neighbors and natural fathers, until now I saw before me the reformer and the bandit, the Genevese and the Scuffletonian in Calvin Oxendine.

He came out from his cell in a greasy

shirt and a pair of woolen trousers belted at the waist, and with his searching, round, indescribable eye, looked me through and through.

It was a black eye, which got its education from a country place where they make an inventory of strangers in the glimpse afforded by a flash of lightning and rob them before the next flash.

The speculation in that pair of eyes that he did glare withal mocked knowledge. It was the gypsy's encyclopedia of a chicken coop, and I was the chicken in view.

From my side of the case it was the worst pair of agates I ever saw—furtive, plaintive, touching, repelling. God save us from these mixed races, that we cannot understand, which civilize themselves on no one line of projection, and give no key to their tortuous character, and are to themselves a heathen mystery!

"I came down the road yesterday, Oxendine, from your part of the world."

The big eyes repeated the performance.

"From Robeson county?"

"Yes."

"Well, did you see that party that went up on Monday—what about them?"

This with a sort of lethargic earnestness, like a sleepy nature slowly rolling out of bed.

"You mean Pop Oxendine?"

"Yes; my brother."

"His trial won't come off for several days. But tell me, Oxendine, how came Henry Berry Lowery to get all you boys in his hands? Has he so much greater power than you, although younger?"

The fellow rolled his orbs at me again, perfectly submissive, but all searching—ignorance and cunning and prowling and wonder reaching out to drink me in and fathom me—and yet, withal, a sort of roadside equality.

His rather over-fed face; his cracked, slipshod shoes; his drooping breeches, were mean enough; but there was the gypsy inquiry nearly *nonchalant*, in his look. Sensual his face certainly was but a deep fallow of power lay in it, generations of the bummer worthy of education from the beginning.

What crimes against human nature have been committed by Southern prejudice against everything with a drop of the negro in it!

This rascal's eye looked like genius more than anything I had seen below Richmond.

"Indeed," he said, after finishing up the study, coolly. "I can't tell you; I don't know anything about it."

Respectful and polite he was all the time, but in his situation, the answer was diplomatic, and the next remark showed that it was not made without logical reference to himself.

"Sheriff, when is my trial coming off. Am I to lie in this dark place two more years?"

"I would insist upon my trial," said the Sheriff.

"I will. "I can't stand it."

Then, after a minute, giving me another roll of his quiet eyes, he said.

"Can you give me a piece of tobacco sir?"

"No; but I can give you the money to get it."

He took it, looked at it, and, pronouncing my name plainly, with thanks although the name had been mentioned only once, walked voluntarily back to his cell.

These mulattoes of the families of Lowery, Oxendine and Strong have been locked away in the fastnesses of a hard Scotch population and their development cramped.

What might have been the discoverer has become the buccaneer; the poet had become the outlaw.

THE SWAMP OUTLAWS.

BLOOD TRAIL.

How Lowery Avenged the Murders of a Father and a Brother—Cain's Brand the Test of Admission to the Gang—A War of Races—The Outlaws in the Swamps—The Judge on the Bench—The Ku klux on Their Nightly Raids—Lowery Breaks Prison Twice—Sheriff King, Norment, Carlisle, Steve Davis and Joe Thompson's Slave Murdered by the Band—Killing the Outlaw's Relatives When They Cannot Catch the Gang—The Ku Klux Under Taylor Slay "Make" Sanderson, Henry Revels and Ben Betha, the Praying Preacher—A Promise That Was Kept—"I will kill John Taylor—There's No Law for Us Mulattoes." Aunt Phœbe's Story—The Hanging of Henderson Oxendine—Outlaw Zach McLaughlin Shot by an Impressed Outlaw—The Black Nemesis.

LUMBARTON, N. C., Feb. 27, 1872.

In two previous letters I have described the persons of the Lowreys and some of their associates, and given the origin of the local feud which has run into an extended career of outlawry and crimes. This letter will recapitulate the leading crimes on both sides, as derived from the best information.

THE TWO ARRESTS AND JAIL-BREAKINGS OF LOWERY.

Although Henry Berry Lowery swore an oath of revenge for the murder of his father and brother in 1865 he was not yet entirely given up to outlawry, and the republican politicians and advisers of the people of Scuffletown felt some sympathy for him and sought to save him. These looked upon the murders of Harris and Barnes as partly justified, in the former case by the monstrous character of the man, in the latter by motives of self-defence and the collisions of the races in the war.

The old slaveholding element of the county, however, unaware of the scourge or humanity they were creating and the talent as an outlaw leader he was to develop, resolved to have and to hang him at all hazards.

They found that he was to be married to Rhody Strong, the most beautiful girl in Scuffletown, and, surrounding the house on the night of the ceremony, they took him from the side of his bride—one A. J. McNair accomplishing his capture. The jail at Lumberton was then in ashes, and the county without a safe receptacle for

THE YOUNG MURDERER AND BRIDEGROOM,

then only twenty years of age. He was therefore conveyed in irons to the jail at Whitesville, Columbus county, twenty-nine miles from Lumberton. Here the desperate young husband filed his way out of the grated iron window bars, escaped to the woods, and made his way back to his wife. This was in 1866.

In the interrupted enjoyment of family happiness Henry Berry Lowery expressed a desire to quit the swamps and return to his carpenter's trade and peaceful society. His republican friends labored again in his behalf, and they resolved to plead the proclamation of oblivion for offences committed during the war, issued by the federal department commanders throughout the South. Dr.

Thomas, Freedmen's Bureau Agent at Scuffletown, arranged with the Sheriff, B. A. Howell, that if Lowery freely gave himself up, he should be well fed, not be put in irons, and protected from the mob. United States troops at that time were quartered throughout North Carolina and the rebel element was discouraged.

The Sheriff and Dr. Thomas called for Lowery at his own cabin, near Asbury church, and brought him into Lumberton in a buggy. A new jail had meantime (1868) been erected in the outskirts of the town, constructed entirely of hewed timber. Lowery was for a time tractable, quiet and confiding in his advisers. The

SULLEN HOSTILITY OF THE TOWNS-PEOPLE—

natural enough, no doubt, toward the murderer of two citizens—soon began to develop, and complaints were made that Lowery had three meals a day, and not two, like the other prisoners. He was fed from the outside by a shoemaker who also acted as jailer, and this good treatment, added to reports of his proud and unintimidated bearing, led to a public cry that he ought to be ironed and put on hard fare. It is charged also —and the story was told to me by three different persons living widely apart— that some of the towns-people, hearing of the line of defence to be assumed for to prisoner, had resolved to drag him from jail and drown him in the river at the foot of the jail-yard hill.

At any rate Lowery grew suspicious and uneasy, and perhaps chafed at confinement. One evening, as the jailer appeared with his food, he presented a knife and a cocked repeater, and said:—

"Look here, I'm tired of this. Open that door and stand aside. If you leave the place for fifteen minutes you will be shot as you come out!"

He then walked out of the jail, turned down the river bank, avoiding the town, stopped at a house and helped himself to some crackers, and, crossing the bridge, was never again seen in Lumberton.

THE BAD CHARACTER COMING OUT.

From that day to this he has led the precarious life of a hunted man and robber, killing sometimes for plunder, sometimes for revenge, sometimes for defence. He has refused to trust any person except those who by bloodshed put themselves out of the pale of society like himself, and he has collected a pack of murderers whom he absolutely commands, and who have finally diminished to five, the rest being sent off as unworthy, useless or uncongenial

"My band is big enough," he said last week. "They are all true men and I could not be as safe with more. We mean to live as long as we can, to kill anybody who hunts us, from the Sheriff down, and at last, if we must die, to die game."

To another person he said. "We are not allowed to get our living peaceably and we must take it from others. We don't kill anybody but the Ku Klux."

A steady moral decline and growing atrocity has been remarked of Henry Berry Lowery, but he has committed no outrages on women and no arsons. His confidence and sense of lonely and desperate independence have become more marked. A cool, murderous humor has gained upon him, and he is a trifle fond of his distinction. Frequent exhibitions of magnanimity distinguish his bloody course and he has learned to arrogate to himself a protectorate over the interests of the mulatoes, which they return by a sort of hero-worship. There is not, probably, a negro in Scuffletown who would betray him, and his prowess is a household word in every black family in sea-board Carolina. His consistent and

UNFLINCHING METHOD OF WARFARE

has gained him awe among the whites, amounting nearly to respect, and by a certain integrity in word and performance he has come to deal with all the community as an absolute and yet not wilful dictator. Like the rattlesnake of the swamps, he sends warning before he kills, and only in robbery is remorseless and sudden.

The family is divided in verdict upon his conduct. Patrick, Sinclair and Purdy, who are Methodists, speak pretty much in these terms (quoted from Patrick Lowery, who is a preacher):—

"My brother Harry had provocation —the same all of us had—when they killed my old father. But he has got to be a bad man, and I pray the Lord to remove him from this world, if he only repent first."

AN ANTE-BELLUM EPISODE.

A good deal of the above is probably deceitful. The current opinion of Scuffletown is as follows, in the language of an aged colored woman at Shoe Heel.

"Massa," she said, "Henry Berry Lowery aint gwying to kill nobody but them that wants to kill him. He's just a paying these white people back for killing his old father, brothers and cousins. His old mother I knew right well, and she says, 'My boys aint doing right, but I can't help it; I can only jiss pray for 'em. They wan't a brought up to do all this misery and lead this yer kind of life.'" "Massta," resumed Aunt Phœbe, "this used to be a dreful hard country for poor niggers. Do you see my teeth up yer, Massta?"

The old woman drew her lip back with her finger and showed the empty gum, with

ONLY A TOOTH AT EACH SIDE.

"My massta—his name's MacQueen (or MacQuade)—knocked 'em all out wid an oak stick. God knows I worked for him wid all my might; but, you see, he was a keepin' black women and his wife gwine to leave him, he wanted me to say she had black men, and I'd a died first! He whipped me and beat me, and at last he struck me wid a stick over de mouf, and, Massta, I jess put up my hand up to catch de blood and all de teef dropped in de palm of my hand. Oh, dis was a hard country, and Henry Berry Lowery's jess a payin' 'em back. He's only a payin' 'em back! It's better days for de brack people now. Massta, he's jess de king o' dis country."

This is a perfectly literal version of a Christian old woman's talk. Bandit and robber as he is, and bloodstained with many murders, this Lowery's crimes scarcely take relief from the blotched background of an intolerant social condition, where the image of God was outraged by slavery through two hundred years of bleeding, suffering and submitting. The black Nemesis is up, playing the Ku Klux for himself, and for many a coming generation the housewives of North Carolina will frighten the children with tales of Lowery's band. Still, the fellow is a cold-blooded, malignant, murderous being, without defenders even among republicans.

MURDER OF SHERIFF REUBEN KING.

The first great crime succeeding the killing of Brant Harris was committed in the motive of house robbery upon a highly esteemed old citizen of advanced years, the Sheriff of Robeson county, Reuben King. This happened on the night of January 23, 1869.

Henry Berry Lowery has since said that he had no intention of accomplishing the death of this gentleman, but that, being poor, and aware that King had a quantity of money in his possession, the "boys" wanted to rob him, and had no notion of putting him out of the world.

After being shot King lingered till the 13th of March, and his antemortem statements, added to the confession of Henderson Oxendine, one of the robbers, give us a complete history of the tragedy. Lowery alleges that he whipped George Applewhite, the negro who fired the fatal shot; but this may be mere cunning, and, besides, the bandits have charged the crime upon John Dial, the State's witness.

The ruffians, hearing that King was possessed of considerable money, came down from Scuffletown and hid in a thicket near his house, which was two miles south of Lumberton. There they built a fire to warm themselves, and, being only partly armed, they cut bludgeons from the swamp and trimmed them.

Dial remarked, "The old Sheriff may resist us!"

"If he does," exclaimed Boss Strong, "we'll kill him!"

They blackened their faces to disguise their identity and race more securely, and then, to the number of eight or nine moved, with the stealth of Indians, up to the dwelling of the hale old gentleman.

Sheriff King was reading the report of a recent Baptist Convention beside his fireplace. In another part of the room—the parlor—Edward Ward, one of his neighbors, who had come to pass the night, was reading a book. Suddenly the door was pushed open and

A ROW OF BLACKENED, HIDEOUS FACES

appeared over the threshold, while a gun barrel was pointed at King, and an imperative voice said:—

"Surrender!"

The man Ward sat as if paralyzed. The Sheriff, roused at the summons from his book, scarcely understood the situation. By a fatal, instinctive movement he leaped up and seized the menacing firearm, and bent it down toward the floor. Henry Berry Lowery, the holder of it, struggled at the butt and bent it up again, and in the wrestle the piece was discharged into the parlor floor, burning and scarring the boards there. By this time the closeness of the encounter and the Sheriff's stiff and powerful hold upon the gun had brought his body around so that his back was toward the open door. At this instant a pistol, at close quarters, was fired into the old man's head from behind, and he fell to the floor in agony. The robbers immediately, and without show of resistance, fired at Edward Ward and felled him with a wound which lasted for months.

The females of the family, rushed in and stood horrified spectators of the misery of the two men. The blackened and excited faces of the robbers struck them with additional terror.

"Water!" gasped the bleeding Sheriff; "I am burning up! For God's sake give me some water!"

"God damn you!" cried one of the villains, "what did you fight for?

"YOU SHAN'T HAVE WATER."

It was a scene of indescribable bloodiness—the screaming women, menaced by the resolute robbers; the groaning victims, the disguised faces of the fiends and their lust for plunder paramount. No wonder that Henry Berry Lowery, ashamed of the remembrance, threatens to shoot any man who says he took part in the performance.

THE HOME-GUARD DEMORALIZED.

After a little time one of the women was allowed to go and get water, while the rest were locked up under guard. Then the robbers ransacked the house, opened trunk after trunk and took some of them out in the yard to investigate their contents. They finally made their escape laden with plunder, and it was not until John Dial pointed out the place where they had cut clubs in the swamp and built the fire that the whole matter was exposed. Dial has now been in jail at Whitesville two years. Two of the persons concerned in this murder have been condemned and escaped, two are in jail and one was hanged.

THE ONLY BANDIT HANGED.

Henderson Oxendine was finally arrested at the house of his brother-in-law, George Applewhite, the negro, while waiting for Mrs. Applewhite to be confined. The authorities, aware of the condition of the culprit's sister, stayed around the house all night and got in at daylight, supposing Applewhite to be there. They at once arrested Henderson Oxendine and Pop Oxendine. The persons named as present at the murder of Sheriff King, in 1869, were John Dial, Stephen Lowery, George Applewhite, Henderson Oxendine, and Calvin Oxendine. These at least were in the custody of the officers at one time, while Henry Berry Lowery, Boss Strong and others also present, were at large.

Steve Lowery and George Applewhite were condemned to be hanged, when, prematurely, the majority of the prisoners, among them the condemned, dug their way out of the prison.

When Henderson Oxendine was hanged there were about thirty-five persons present in the small jail yard, but the tree tops overlooking the enclosure were filled with whites and negroes.

The gallows was of the rudest contruction, built against the high picket fence of the jail, with a trap, which was held up by a rope passing over the short beam secured, behind the upright joist by a wooden clamp, so that it could be severed by the blow of a hatchet. Oxendine's mother came to the jail the morning of the execution and condoled with her boy.

He was a thin-jawed, columnar-necked wild, whitish mulatto, with ears set back like a keen dog's, a good forehead, piercing, almost staring round eyes, with dark, barbaric lights in them, a nose eminent for its alert nostril, and a longish, near bottomed chin, set with thin, dirtyish beard, and a mouth of African suggestion.

Pride and stoicism were in his expression, and negro-like, he sung a couple of hymns on the gallows out of the Baptist collection.

His executioner was a Northern rough named Marden, or Marsden, a waif from somewhere, who resembled a sailor's boarding house runner, and was of lower estate than the Lowerys.

This is one of the beings who has rung himself in on the people of Robeson county, ostensibly as a detective. He pinioned Oxendine and then severed the supporting rope with the hatchet.

No attempt at rescue was made.

THE MURDER OF OWEN C. NORMENT.

The first murder committed in cold blood for revenge was upon the person of Owen C. Norment, who lived four miles from the hut of Henry Berry Lowery and eight miles from Red Banks station. His house was also three miles from Alfordsville, on the road to Lumberton, and not far from the dwelling of a white desperado called Zach McLaughlin. Aaron Swamp, a feeder of Back Swamp, was near Norment's house. This murder was committed by Zach McLaughlin, by order of Henry Berry Lowery, who, with his command, was posted near. It was the first white man killed by the gang since 1864, a lapse of more than five years.

Norment was an overbearing ex-slaveholder, who had shot a man dead at Charlotte, N. C., for calling him a liar, and had been tried for it and acquitted.

He had very black hair, whiskers and eyes, and weighed about one hundred and sixty-five pounds.

His offence was raising the people against the Lowerys, charging robberies to them and threatening them.

Hearing loud noises, as of the stirring up of domestic animals, the rattling of wagon chains, &c., outside of his house.

Norment walked out in the dusk of a Saturday evening and asked who was present. Hearing somebody moving in the dusk, he called for his wife to give him his gun.

Almost immediately a gun was fired only ten feet from Norment and he was shattered in the lower members and elsewhere with shot and ball.

He fell instantly, and being removed to the house, a servant was despatched for a physician.

Dr. Dick obeyed the summons, and being driven in a mule buggy by one Bridgers, they were greeted, one mile from Norment's house, with a discharge of firearms, which killed the mule and forced the driver and the doctor to take to the woods.

The same night Archie Graham, a neighbor, was shot and dangerously wounded, and also Ben MacMillan, another obnoxious personage.

The house of a Mr. Jackson, on the Elizabeth road, was also fired into and his dog killed.

The robbers held carnival that night and resumed the reign of terror.

Norment's leg was amputated, but the doctor was nervous, as the wounds were fatal, for he died on Monday morning, thirty-six hours after being shot, leaving a wife and three children.

THE MURDER OF JOE THOMPSON'S SLAVE.

The Lowerys had once been slaveholders, and Henry Berry always refers to the full blacks as "niggers."

A good while prior to the time of the killing of O. C. Norment the Lowery gang shot dead a negro belonging to one Joe Thompson, who lived at Ashpole Swamp, sixteen miles from Lumberton, and was a neighbor of Henry Berry Lowery.

The band had robbed Thompson's house of bedclothing, &c., and, thinking of some story relative to their doings which the negro had told, they shot him dead at his own shanty.

Then they ordered Thompson's driver to gear up the family carriage and drive them home, which he did, and they left the vehicle not far from Henry Berry Lowery's house.

This must have been about at the close of the war, for the driver narrates that three United States deserters or escaped prisoners were then with the mulatto robbers.

THE FATE OF ZACH M'LAUGHLIN.

This Zach McLaughlin, who is alleged to have inflicted the mortal wound upon Mr. Norment, met with a fate justly deserved.

He was a native of Scotland, and one of a low, sensual, heathenish type of white men who consorted with mulattoes and spent his low energies in seducing mulatto girls and women.

Having laid out in the swamps with the Strongs, Lowerys and Applewhite, he picked up an almost equally renegade white by the name of Biggs, when, one evening, the twain met at a mulatto shanty upon an identical object—namely a mulatto syren.

As they quitted the place to go home McLaughlin, who was drinking deeply of villanous liquor, said to Biggs, with an oath:—

"I'll kill you right here unless you join with me and rob the smokehouses and shanties of some of these freedmen. We want you with our crowd, and you've got to come or die."

Biggs says in his statement that he went, out of the fear of death, and helped in the robberies of that night, but privately made up his mind to escape from McLaughlin or to kill him.

McLaughlin finally grew very drunk, and insisted upon building a fire at a place in the swamp and resting there.

These two men were now quite separated from other companionship, and when the fire was lighted, McLaughlin, who possessed a monopoly of the arms, compelled Biggs to sleep between himself and the burning brands, while he, meantime, bent akimbo over the burning blaze and dozed.

Biggs began to test the sleeping outcast by rolling and moving, and finally by jostling McLaughlin.

Remembering his description of his pistols, and in particular one pistol, which was described as

NEVER MISSING FIRE.

Biggs managed to pull it from the sheath in McLaughlin's belt. With this he shot the white outlaw through and through and then slipped away into the swamp to see if he moved.

The drunken beast being perfectly dead, Biggs made his way to Lumberton and related the story. Search was made, and on the spot of ground indicated, beside the extinguished fire, the bloody carcass of McLaughlin was discovered.

Just previous to this affair—November 9, 1871—McLaughlin and Tom Lowery had escaped from Lumberton jail by availing themselves of a loose iron bar and wrenching the grates off the jail windows.

Biggs received $400 for his two shots into McLaughlin's body.

He has figured in a subordinate degree since that time as a volunteer to capture the outlaw chief.

McLaughlin was altogether a meaner specimen of mankind than the Strongs and Lowerys.

THE MURDER OF STEVE DAVIS.

On the 3d of October, 1870, the Lowery band of outlaws appeared at the house of Angus Leach, near Floral College (female), and proceeded to seize a large quantity of native brandy, distilled there for the fruit-growing neighbors—some say brandy designed to to evade the revenue laws.

Lowery's band was alert and fond of strong drink, and they seized all the available vessels at hand—kegs, pitchers, pots and measures—to transport the liquor.

Unwilling to despoil without inflicting pain, they struck old Angus Leach over the hip with a gun stock, disabling him, and a negro man, showing some solicitude for the fluid property, they tied up, whipped him with a wagon trace and slit his ears with a penknife.

The liquor which they did not remove they destroyed before the United States revenue officer could find it.

Next night the persons who had placed their fruit, &c., for distillation at this place, started in pursuit of the fugitives.

They found the whole party, very drunk, at George Applewhite's, between Red Banks and Plumer's station.

Applewhite was an alert, thick-lipped deep-browed, woolly headed African, with a steadfast, brutal expression.

Firing into the house the outlaws rushed out, well armed and spoiling for a fight. The neighbors wounded nearly every man of the party.

Boss Strong was shot in the forehead, Henderson Oxendine in the arm and George Applewhite in the thigh.

Steve O. Davis, of Moore county, a fine young man and brave as youth dare be, rushed ahead of the party and forced the fighting in the swampy edge of the field where the outlaws were.

Henry Berry Lowery took deliberate sight upon him and shot him through the back of the head. He fell dead.

THE MURDER OF CARLISLE.

I possesss no data upon the murder of a Mr. Carlisle, who appears to have been killed in the early part of the open and announced warfare, except the record that some of the bobtail followers of Lowery's band were accused of the crime.

One "Shoemaker John," not proven guilty of the murder of Mr. Carlisle, received a sentence of ten years in the State Penitentiary March 1, 1871, for burglary. He appeared to be glad of the opportunity to go safely to jail and to escape, on the one hand, the mob, and on the other the Lowery gang.

"DAL BAKER."

In the fall of 1866 Daniel or "Dal" Baker was shot in the leg while near Scuffletown, and his leg had to be amputated.

Several other shootings occurred about this time, and the war being now well understood, the citizens, volunteers, militia and two companies of United States troops started in to make a set campaign against the outlaws.

Here some atrocities were committed properly belonging to this narrative.

Among the crimes of the Lowery band must be placed in legitimate context some of the more precipitate crimes committed against the mulatoes of Scuffletown by their white neighbors.

Eight negroes have been killed by the whites episodically in the hunts for the Lowerys.

THE MURDER OF BEN BETHA.

Ben Betha was a full-blooded negro and a violent radical republican among his color, and he was used by the republican politicians to disseminate their doctrines and keep the color in Scuffletown united in vote and sentiment.

He was what is called a praying politician, apt to be frenzied and loud in prayer and to exhort wildly, and he has cunning enough to ring politics and the wrongs of the colored people into his prayers, so that he might have been said to pray the whole ticket.

Last winter the democrats having full possession of the county, and the Ku Klux going barefaced and undisguisedly through Samson, Richmond and the adjoining counties, it was resolved to make an example of this praying negro.

The Coroner of the county, Robert Chaafin, got a party ostensibly to hunt for Lowery, he being the pretext for all Ku Klux operations in Robeson, and it is alleged that some members of the party came out of Battery A. United States artillery, then posted in and about Scuffletown.

THE ROBESON COUNTY KU KLUX seldom wore disguises, the Lowery pretext covering all their operations.

With eighteen young men they started towards Ben Betha's and the proposition was then sprung to take him out and kill him that night.

Alarmed at this, Chaafin, the MacQueens, and some of the more prudent turned back, afraid of Judge Russell's bench warrants. Malcolm MacNeil now took command, and, at the head of ten men, marched up to Ben Betha's door between twelve and one o'clock, and rapping there, said to the negro as he appeared:—

"Come out here! We want you." The darky seemed aware by their resolute faces that his hour, long threatened, had come, and he turned about and said to his wife—"Ole woman, I specs they's gwine to kill me. Mebbe I'll never come back no mo'."

"Go and get your hat!" was the next order, and then the negro was lifted out of the shanty, and for one quarter of a mile there was no sign of his well known foot tracks.

The fact was that he had been lifted on a horse and ridden off a quarter of a mile, so as to hide his traces. The tracks reappeared after a certain distance and the negro was never more heard of after that night, but was found dead, shot through and through.

Judge Russell called upon the Grand Jury to indict every man of this party; but the Grand Jury, with that provebial Southern justice manifested towards the negro,

IGNORED THE BILL,

and then the Judge, with almost extra judicial severity, put his written protest on the records of the Court, and denounced the action of the Grand Jury as outrageous.

He then issued his bench warrant, and outlawed every man concerned in the killing of Betha, and they all ran out of the county.

Malcolm MacNiel went to Baltimore, where he is a clerk in a store, and his brother has fled to Mississippi. This happened only a few months ago.

The negro waiter in the hotel at Lumberton said to me in the presence of several white men of the town :—

"They say they go up to Scuffletown to hunt Lowery; but I never knew them to go there without killing some innocent person."

THE MURDER OF HENRY REVELS.

The murder of Henry Revels, a mulatto boy, is another case in point. One night Dr. Smith, north of Scuffletown, came into that settlement and said he had been shot at on the road by somebody.

Dr. Smith was a brother of Colonel Smith, the democratic Treasurer of the county, and also a merchant at Shoe Heel.

Putting their heads together the Shoe Heelers concluded that the fellow was Henry Revels, a likely mulatto, who had become a leading republican and was somewhat saucy around that region.

He had been brought up by Hugh Johnson and made a body servant, so that he had a better appearance and more intelligence than the ordinary run of Scuffletowners.

Fifteen or sixteen men on horseback and in buggies started out from Shoe Heel and rode six miles off, to Johnson's place, and took young Revels by force out of the house, telling him not to open his mouth.

They carried him to the vicinity of Floral College, where resided the Rev. Mr. Coble, chaplain on the occasion of the killing of old Allen Lowery.

There Revels was shot dead and his carcass thrown behind a woodpile. The negroes found the carcass and called up the reverend divine to identify it.

Coble, by this time not anxious to fall into the hands of Judge Russell, had the Coroner cited, but before a jury could be summoned some person concerned in the murder took the body and hid it in a mudhole, where the negroes again discovered it and the inquest was held.

Warrants were issued for these Ku Klux, and put in the hands of John Mac Niell, of Smith township, the constable there, but he failed to do his duty and all the parties ran away.

THE OXENDINES SHOT AND WHIPPED.

This MacNeil, although a constable and head of the militia in his township, was personally concerned in the outrage on the Oxendines.

Hearing that Tom Lowery, one of the outlaws, was dead, and wishing to prove it and discover the body, perhaps for the purpose of getting the reward, it was resolved to pay the Oxendines a visit.

They went to the house of Jesse Oxendine, son of John, who was working quietly at turpentine-making, and MacNiell said :—

"Where is Tom Lowery buried?"

John Oxendine replied that he did not know, and was not aware that he was dead.

The constable's posse then put a strap around the neck of Oxendine, and, passing it over the limb of a tree, hung him up but the man's weight broke the limb. They hung him to a second limb, but the sapling bent toward the ground.

Then they put the strap around his neck so that the ends hung over, and two men pulled it each way until the negro grew black in the face.

Nearly at the same time they shot another of the Oxendines, at his own gate-post through both hands.

Bench warrants were issued, but they could not have them served by the Sheriff or the United States officers, and the fifteen or twenty men concerned in the outrage went out of the county for a while until the thing blew over.

In this brutal way the hunt for Henry Berry Lowery goes on, and the people who cannot catch him revenge themselves upon his neighbors.

THE MURDER OF "MAKE" SANDERSON.

The murder of Make Sanderson— Make meaning Malclom—would have been fully investigated had it not been for the fact that Tom Russell, a brother of the republican Judge Russell, was one of the party who murdered him and the Judge let the subject drop on that account.

Make Sanderson was a mulatto of such light skin that before the war he enjoyed the general privilege of whites.

He married a sister of Henderson Oxendine, who was afterwards hanged at Lumberton. Sanderson's wife being also the daughter of John Oxendine, who was a half brother of old Allen Lowery, father of the Lowery gang.

There appears to have been nothing charged against Make Sanderson except his relationship by marriage to the Lowery family.

It is generally asserted that he was a harmless man, "bossed" by his wife. On one of the periodical futile raids for Henry Lowery the militia, or the volunteers, among whom was Murdoch MacLain John Taylor, the Pursells, Tom Russell and others, arrested Make Sanderson and Andrew Strong, and, tying their wrists together so tightly that the blood came, marched them to the house of Mr. Inman, a republican and father of the boy afterwards

KILLED BY THE LOWERYS.

At Inman's they got a plough line, and, tying the two more securely, then marched the pair to John Taylor's who lived about two miles from Moss Neck.

As John Taylor had gone over to the house of his father-in-law, William C. MacNiell, the march was continued to that point, and here, in the dusk, the party stopped in MacNiell's lane, sending messages to and fro until dark.

The object of this was to keep the crime within the circle and not put the MacNiells in danger of Henry Berry Lowery's vengeance.

While the negroes were led together Andrew Strong, certain that he was going to be shot, gave his penknife to Ben Strickland, another negro, and told him to give it to his wife, because it was all that he had in the world, and he should never see her again.

This latter point came out as circumstantial evidence, because afterwards John Taylor attempted to deny that he ever had Andrew Strong in custody when he was brought before the Court for the murder of Make Sanderson.

At dark both negroes were brought up to William C. MacNiell's yard, and all the party of capturers took food on the piazza, and while there John Taylor, a black-eyed, black-haired, bearded, resolute man and the most determined hunter that ever started against the Lowerys, walked out of the house upon the piazza.

Both the negroes fell on their knees

and held up their hands, bound as they were, and cried:—

"O, Mr. Taylor, save my life! Save my life!"

A KU KLUX NERO.

Taylor drew back with his foot half raised, as if about to kick them, and he said, bitterly:—

"If all the mulatto blood in the country was in you two, and with one kick I could kick it out, I would send you all to hell together with my foot."

The negroes were then taken across MacNeill's dam, where John Taylor, within a few weeks, was to fall dead with the roof of his head shot off, and marched to the woods north of Moss Neck station, about one mile, until the party reached a sort of wild dell in the lonely country.

John Taylor did not accompany the party, but the two MacNeills did, and also Murdoch MacLain, Tom Russell, some of the Pursells and John Paterson, of Richmond county.

Andrew Strong, who afterwards related these incidents to his lawyer, says that himself and Make Sanderson were now made to stand up together, asked if they had anything to say, because they had now got to die, and with this their hats were pulled down over their eyes with an ostentation of pity. Murdoch MacLain, who appeared to be the captain, then cried out:—

"The shooting party will be Nos. 1, 2, and 3. Step out!"

Andrew Strong asserts that No. 2 was "Sandy" MacNeil, brother-in-law of John Taylor.

Make Sanderson, who appeared perfectly resigned, asked if they would give him time to pray.

After a little conference the answer was:—"Yes, you may pray."

Strong says that Make Sanderson then fell on his knees and made the most wonderful prayer that he ever heard in his life, the woods ringing with his loud, frenzied utterances as he spoke of his wife and children, and finally, negro fashion, he became so earnest that one of the fellows, who had a towel wrapped around his head—so had the majority—stepped up and hit Sanderson with the butt of a pistol, saying.

"Shut up, you damned nigger! You shan't make any such noise as this if you are going to be shot!"

AFTER THE PRAYER,

there was some little delay among the assassins.

Some of them were evidently growing frightened between the prospects of vengeance from Sanderson's connections and Judge Russell's Court.

This interval Andrew Strong improved to loosen, little by little, the rope which tied his wrists to Sanderson's and suddenly getting his hand out he rushed into the woods and ran like a deer.

They riddled the woods with buckshot and ball, but never saw him again until he appeared against John Taylor and others in the Court at Lumberton.

The remaining negro, who exhibited no desire to run, being a weak fellow without much stamina, was taken back to the mill dam by MacNiell's house, for the party had lost spirits and feared that the other negro would inform upon them.

Here, it is said, they consulted with John Taylor, who said that indecision would do no good, and that now the negro had better be killed, since his companion would spread the tidings.

For two days Make Sanderson was not seen. John Taylor and all the band denied having encountered him at all.

A negro found him below the mill tail, in the swamp place behind the mill,

A SPY CAUGHT BY THE LOWERY BANDITS.

shot in the abdomen with a great quantity of buckshot, and then again shot in the back of the neck, in such close quarters that his hair was burned as by the flash of a pistol.

The man looked as if he had first been shot and then endeavored to grope his way up out of the water, for the palms of his hands and fingers were torn.

The body was deposited in MacNiell's mill and then hastily buried, but the Magistrate of Lumberton, Parson Sinclair, had it disinterred and the inquest held.

The verdict was, "Shot by parties unknown to the jury."

Magistrate Sinclair issued warrants for the leaders in this affair, and sent them to prison without bail; but Judge Russell, notwithstanding the high nature of his offence, released John Taylor on a bond of $500, supposedly because Tom Russell was in the transaction.

When Henry Berry Lowery heard that John Taylor was out on $500 bail, and that this was considered security enough for the murder of his relative, he said—

"WELL, I WILL KILL JOHN TAYLOR there is now no law for us mulattoes."

Three weeks afterwards, as John Taylor crossed the mill dam, coming down from the house of his father-in-law to the station, the gang of outlaws rose from the swamp within thirty yards of the place where Sanderson had been killed, and Henry Berry Lowery shot the skull and brains out of Taylor and then robbed him of his pocketbook

Thus perished a man brave, zealous, active and a good citizen to all but negroes, whom, with the old-fashioned contempt for slaveholders, he regarded, in the language of Judge Taney, as "without rights that white men were bound to respect."

Here my letter exceeds bounds, and I will try to finish up the bloody recapitulation in one more article.

THE MULATTO CAPITAL.

Origin of the Free Negro Settlement. First Appearance of the Lowery Half-Breeds The Old Tuscarora Blood. Life and Feeling in Scuffletown. Cause of the Vendetta. Lowery's Cousins Slain by Brant Harris. The Murder of Barnes and Harris. Old Allen Lowery and Bill Lowery Shot by the Home Guard. The Vow of Revenge. Abortive Efforts to Make Peace. The Lowerys Exempted From the Act of Oblivion.

LUMBERTON, N. C., FEB. 26, 1872.

Here is the place where the Lowery gang has been in jail, whence futile processes are issued for them, and where any of the members ever caught will be hanged or burned.

It is a town almost wholly built of unpainted planks or logs, which have become nearly black with weather stains. The streets are sandy and without pavements of either brick or wood.

About nine hundred people reside in the place, and nearly every white man in it and in the surrounding country is Scotch.

The country was settled by Scotch Highlanders before the Revolution, and afterwards by a promiscuous emigration from the west coast of Scotland.

About thirty miles distant, at Fayetteville, lived Donald and Flora MacDonald, the latter the savior of Prince Charles, the Pretender; the former the defeated champion of the royal standard at the beginning of our war of independence.

These Scotch slaveholders were hard task masters, and they look with pinched and awry faces upon the negro voting beside them.

The county government is democratic, and so perfectly impotent to catch or kill five outlaws that at present it is making no exertions whatever.

Indeed, the opinion prevails that the Sheriff's office has concluded a truce upon what are called honorable terms with Henry Berry Lowery.

If it can be said that these bandits are republicans it must also be charged that the county government is democratic, and the honors are easy between pillage and impotence.

COURT SCENES AT LUMBERTON.

The Court House is built of brick, with a frame pediment above the eaves in the gable end, and the court room in the second story is covered with sawdust to keep the peace while Judge Clarke, one of the District Judges, goes through the comedy of justice.

"Make proclamation!" cries he, or his clerk, to the Sheriff, who stands at an open window opposite the bench, and who roars down in a stentorian way to the people assembled in the public area: "Neil Mc Neil! Campbell McGregor! McLeod Duncan! come into court, as you are this day commanded, or your security will be forfeited to the State!"

This kind of noise, with variations of "Oh, yes! Oh, yes!" goes on pretty much all day, while witnesses, jurors and attached people are being summoned.

The court room is very crude, large and bare, and the Judge looks amazingly high up behind the long gallery where they expose him.

He is a queer, affable old Judge, who has fought in the Mexican war, in the Confederate army, and commanded one of Holden's regiments (Kirk leading the other) against the Ku Klux.

He is at present what is called a "scalawag," and says, among many other things of no consequence, that if he ever sees Lowery he will kill him. The opportunities appear good for this sort of intention.

Down before the Court House, where the people of the county are congregated, there is an old pole well in the public square, where white and negro fill their gourds at the dripping bucket.

Around the corner stands the old dray—curious vehicle for such a village—on which the Lowery band hauled off a safe from the rear of a Lumberton store, deliberately backing the dray up through an alley between two houses and leisurely setting the valuable casket thereon, stopping at the Court House, with a contempt of superstition, to haul off the county safe.

To do all this required the opening of a man's stable, stealing his horse and the robbing of a blacksmith's shop of tools to break open the safes, as well as the impressment of an additional pair of wagon wheels to convey the larger safe to the woods. The horse could not pull the whole load, and the county safe was dropped off within town limits. The valiant volunteers and posse of the Sheriff marched out of town two or three miles and found the private safe rifled of about twenty-seven thousand dollars.

This was money which had been placed in the hands of the safe-owner for private keeping. Strange as it may seem, this robbery caused a feeling of relief in many minds.

With so great a quantity of money it was hoped that Lowery's band might have quitted the country, and such riddance would have been cheaply purchased at the figure named.

LIFE AT THE BELEAGUERED TOWN.

The tavern at Lumberton is without a sign-post, and is a weather-stained frame house, with small bedrooms, no carpets, no bar and a fair country table.

I found no milk to drink with coffee anywhere in the region, but plenty of eggs and chickens.

The jail—not on the same site where Henry Berry Lowery was once confined, and whence several of the outlaws effected their escape—is truly a singular edifice.

It is built in a grove of oaks and pines in the environs of the town, and constructed wholly of hewn timber, enclosed by a high paling picket fence, outside of which picket is a log guard house for small offenders.

I stepped inside the jail yard, nobody objecting, to make a sketch of the gallows where Henderson Oxendine recently met his fate stoically, no rescue attempted, only the singing of a couple of voluntary hymns himself, negro fashion.

The cord supporting the drop was not severed by the Sheriff, but a desperado from Ohio voluntarily assumed the office.

While I sat within the sloping jail yard I heard a banjo "tumming" in the jail, and the negroes confined there were comparing with Pop Oxendine and the newly arrived offenders for Wilmington the relative quality of meals vouchsafed at the two prisons.

The Lumber River, which flows into the Little Pedee, of South Carolina, and reaches the sea near Georgetown, is at this time of the year little wider than a city street, and of running water, but barely fordable and capable of carrying logs and rafts of lumber down the six score miles of its course.

Hearing horrible imprecations made on the other side of the river, accompanied by cries of "Give me my knife! Yes, I'll cut his heart out! I say gi'e me my knife! My blood's been insulted. A man of hono' can't live after he's been kicked out o' that court room!" &c., &c.,

I was relieved to find that it was merely a negro lad, rejoicing in his rights as a freeman, who wanted to escape, Lowery-fashion, from his mother and brother, and vent his whiskey courage upon somebody.

There are many negroes, as I found, whose freedom takes the form of boasting and cursing.

I failed to perceive in the attorneys and merchants of Lumberton any particular crudeness or inferiority.

Judge Leech and several others were representative men of good sense, but of strong, unmanageable political and social prejudices, and they have succeeded in segregating and solidifying the negro vote, so that the two faces may about be said to make the two political parties.

Here, in the large and motley crowd assembled to attend Court, were to be seen the rival elements of this provicial population.

The whites generally wore butternut, copperas-colored or gray home-spun stuff and large-rimmed, flat, stiff felt hats.

Many of them were very ignorant and could not read, and looked upon the Court as the very judgment seat of Cæsar.

"You just stand up and when your name is called you say 'guilty' and pay your money," I heard a lawyer say to a boor. The boor looked as if it required vast heroism to say even as much

THE SCUFFLETOWNERS AT COURT.

Here, also, were the Scuffletown mulattoes—that curious race—imposed upon for many generations by master and slave, their husbands cuckolded their women debased and intimidated, their freedom not worthy of the name.

Had Robeson county exerted decent endeavors to protect these immemorial free people, when slavery was the law and the horrible radical had not yet subverted "the constitution" which few of the folks who weep for it ever read, or, reading, respected — this existing outlawry would have been precluded.

Scuffletown, over whose name and etymology there seems to be debate, possibly got its name from the long scuffle of the whites and the slaves to reduce it to peonage and make freedom under the condition of color, contemptible among the mulattoes.

Nobody in the whole region could account for this free negro settlement—one of two large aggregations of yellow men which has existed in North Carolina since the organization of society.

There were many theories, but no reasons at hand for them.

I conceive that these negroes might have been the slaves of tories driven from the State at the close of the Revolution, or of the emancipated slaves of the Quakers, and that they increased and multiplied by accessions from runaways, by the birth rate of force exerted on them and by the necessity of union or the sympathy of all neighboring free negroes with a homogeneous settlement.

The comely mulatto women, the strange mulatto men, both sexes decently clad, were plentiful in town—some arriving on mule back, some in short, homemade carts, many on foot.

There was a good deal of drinking among the men and of covert courtship and ogling among the girls. Virtue was evidently not uniformly high in Scuffletown.

SCUFFLETOWN TOPOGRAPHICALLY.

The Rutherford and Wilmington Railroad runs westward from Lumberton River.

Eight miles northwestward it strikes the station of Moss Neck. Seven miles from Moss Neck it strikes the station of Red Banks.

These two stations bound Scuffletown, which spreads besides three or four miles on both sides of the track, and is surrounded on three sides with swamps, which send branches of swamp up through it, and in wet weather each of these swamps are receivers of supplies "bays," bottoms, or pools, which permeate the mulatto fortress.

In fact, it is a part of the "great swamp district of North and South Carolina, below the terrace of hills, and yet is nothing particularly frightful, even to a stranger, and quite unlike our notion of the swamps of Florida and Louisiana.

These swamps enclose the rivers and their arteries laterally for a few yards, and often, or generally, as the stream winds, there is swamps on one side and low clay sandbluffs opposite. It is a mean country for troops to trespass upon, but not an impregnable country.

I believe that I am safe in saying that no Northern society would plead this region as excuse for not following up and annihilating such a crowd as Lowery's band.

THE LAND OF LOWERY.

Taking the railroad as the axis of reference, and looking away from Lumberton northwestward, we see Raft Swamp leave the river first, and after six or seven miles incursion northward, send on, parallel with the railroad on the right, Burnt Swamp, Panther Swamp, and Richland Swamp, extensions of each other. On this side of the track Lowery's band have never committed a murder, unless they killed the McLeods.

Two or three miles above Raft Swamp —the river bending to the right of the track—the Lumber River, itself swamp girt, sends off at opposite sides Bear Swamp (for Jack's Branch), which encloses Moss Neck and Bule's stations, and Back Swamp, which lies about paralled with the Lumber for twenty miles, and projects to the southward Ashpole Swamp and Aaron Swamp.

Here, then, are four series of swamps, counting the swampy Lumber River. The swamps are only a mile or two apart and their feeders diminish the distance. On Back Swamp the Lowery band keeps its ambush and secret camps.

The Lumber River is his line of defence from the railway. The swamps around Moss Neck are the scenes of its boldest assassinations. The house of Henry Berry Lowery, the leader, is beyond Back Swamp, five miles from Moss Neck station, and covered in the rear by Ashpole and Aaron Swamps, and all Scuffletown is his political ally and "boozing ken."

The operations directed against him start from Lumberton on the east and Shoe Heel on the west, twenty-one miles apart, and each twelve miles from his fastness. Further in his rear, on the South Carolina side, the Little Pedee as well, send up parallels of swamp. Florence, a great prison pen for federal troops in the war is fifty miles behind him.

As old Aunt Phœbe said to me at Shoe Heel.

"Boss, Henry Berry Lowery is de king o' the country"

SCUFFLETOWN AS A DEFENSIVE TRACT.

The free negroes settled upon the Scuffletown tract because the poverty of the soil and the half inundated condition of the region brought it within their means and debarred it from the capacity of white men.

In wet weather, after rains, when the Lumber River and its tributaries rise, this region is almost flooded, and then the only means of inter-communication are small paths, known only to the inhabitants, which connect the island-like patches and afford a labyrinthian, mazes for escape to any who keep the clues.

The Lumber River has bridges at but one or two points, and, being swift and deep, must be crossed by scows or rafts.

In summer a luxuriant undergrowth covers all the swamps and low places, and even the prairie pine land, so that one cannot see his own length, while in winter the streams are full of water and the swamps more extensive.

The gallberry tree, sweet gums, post oak, hickory, cypress and all the pine varieties, grow in the swamps and on their margins, and the bamboo vine, stretching out eccentrically and profligately, makes a nearly impenetrable abatis.

The serpents are numerous and often dangerous, including every variety of the moccasin, the rattlesnake and the largest specimens of water and black snakes known in temperate regions.

Lizards live in the decaying logs, and snapping turtles appear in the pools, creeks and bays.

The woods are plentifully supplied with wild cats, which kill pigs and lambs; and the silence of the night in the reptilian region is broken by the great ill-omened owl, which utters no mere "tu-whit," but appals the silence with his long foreboding note, like the very demon of the woods mourning for prey.

A TOUR OF SCUFFLETOWN.

The stranger who expects to see in Scuffletown any approach to a municipal settlement will be disappointed.

It is the name of a tract of several miles, covered at wide intervals with hills and log cabins of the rudest and simplest construction, sometime a half dozen of these huts being proximate.

Two or three places to sell a low character of spirits exist where the dwellings are densest. The people have few or no horses, but often keep a kind of stunted ox to haul their short, rickety carts, and a man with such a bovine hubin and a pair of old wheels is esteemed rich; yet, living upon such land and for so many years, the mulatoes of Scuffletown would have esteemed themselves well to do had they enjoyed any security from their white neighbors. They had little more equity before a jury than negroes, and it was no great offence to violate their asylums and court their wives and daughters.

The whole Lowery war afterward began with Brant Harris' keeping in a sort of servile concubinage some girls courted by the Lowerys.

To visit a Scuffletown shanty, representative of the whole, is to pass by a cow lane or foot track up through a thicket and suddenly come upon a half-cleared field of old pine and post oak, enclosed by a worm fence without a gate.

A little old lever-well of the crudest

mechanism—seldom of the dignity and proportions of a pole well—stands in this lot, the male proprietor of which is sitting on the worm fence, and he replies to your neighborly salutation without changing his position.

Advancing, to the cabin it is found built of hewn logs, morticed at the ends the chinks stopped with mud, the chimney built against one gable on the outside, of logs and clay, with sticks and clay above, where it narrows to the smoke hole.

There is beside the large chimney place, a half barrel, sawed off, to make lye from the wood ashes, and the other half of the barrel is seen to serve the uses of a washtub.

A mongrel dog is always a feature of the establishment. The two or three acres of the lot are generally ploughed and planted in potatoes or maize, both of which come up sickly.

The yellow woman commonly has a baby at the breast, and from half a dozen to a dozen playing outside on the edges of the swamp.

The bed is made on the floor; there are two or three stools; only one apartment comprising the whole establishment.

LOWERY'S CABIN.

Just such a place as the above is the house of Henry Berry Lowery, the outlaw chief, except that, being a carpenter he has nailed weather strips over the interstices between the logs and made himself a sort of bedstead and some chairs.

His cabin has two doors, opposite each other, in the sides, and it has been so many times shot through and through with rifle balls that his wife can now stand fire as well as her husband.

The Scuffletowners go out to work as ditchers for the neighboring farmers, who pay them the magnanimous wages of $6 a month.

As many of them are intemperate a neighboring trader with a barrel of molasses and a barrel of rum speedily gets the $6 from the whole party.

The above picture while true of the majority of the Scuffletowners, is not justly descriptive of all.

The Oxendines are all well to do, or were before this bloody fend began, and the Lowerys were industrious carpenters, whose handiwork is seen at Lumberton, Shoe Heel and all round that region

Great crimes in Scuffletown were rare before the war.

Petty stealing and pilfering of chickens and an occasional pig were not unknown.

The whites hated the settlement because it was a bad example to the negroes. But most of the people were Baptists or Methodists, and nearly all owned their homesteads.

RISE OF SCUFFLETOWN.

By the census of 1860 Robeson county contained 8,459 whites, only three free blacks, all males, and the extraordinary number of 1,459 free mulattoes. There were only 113 foreigners.

But one county—Halifax—contained so many free mulattoes, and that was the county whence the grandfather of the present outlaws of Robeson emigrated.

In 1860 there were 2,165 mulattoes and 287 free blacks in Halifax. Wake county had next below Robeson 1,196 mulattoes, and after Hertford county, with 1,020. There were no counties in all the State with more than a few hundred; the average was not above fifty to each county.

At the same time Robeson county had 126 slave mulattoes and 5,329 slave

THE SWAMP OUTLAWS. 45

ADVANCE OF THE TROOPS INTO THE SWAMPS.

blacks. Altogether the county contained 15,489 souls, the free population making almost two-thirds.

It stood considerably above the average counties of the State in slaves and population, and out of the full-blooded Indians (1,158 in number) ascribed to North Carolina, none were set down either to Robeson or Halifax county.

The antiquity of these free negro settlements might be inferred from the fact that by the census of 1830 only two slaves were manumitted that year. In 1860 there were manumitted 258, or one out of every 1,283.

In the latter year there were 5,262 fugitives from North Carolina to 17,501 from South Carolina.

Where did the South Carolina fugitives hide?

Perhaps no inconsiderable portion of them sought the swamp counties on the southern tier of North Carolina, and begged the charity of this large free negro settlement.

THE INDIAN RACE OF THE LOWERYS.

The question ensues, whence came the Indian blood of the Lowerys? who are by general assertion and belief partly of Indian origin.

Why should they and their blood relatives show Indian traces while Scuffletown at large is mainly plain, unromantic mulatto?

There were two sets of aboriginese in North Carolina—the Cherokees of the west, mountainous Carolina, who removed at a comparatively recent period to the Indian Territory and of whom several remnants remain in the extreme western corner or pocket of the State, numbering 1,062 in Jackson county alone.

Judge Leech, of Lumberton, says that he saw a Cherokee once who resembled Patrick Lowery so closely that he called out, "Is that Patrick?"

Besides the Cherokees there was the Atlantic coast confederacy, led by the Tuscaroras and abetted at the great massacre of 1711 by the Hatteras Indians, the Pamilicos and the Cothechneys.

These Indians, after a determined resistance to the whites, which resulted in scaring the Baron de Graff, the Swiss founder of Newbern, out of the New World, accepted a reservation of lands in Halifax and Bertie counties, near the Roanoke River.

They emigrated to New York and joined the Five Nations a few years afterward, being thought worthy in prowess to be admitted to that proud confederacy, but they held the fee simple of their lands in North Carolina until after the year 1840.

Some persons of the tribe must have remained behind to look after these lands, and among these, as will be seen hereafter, was the grandfather of the Lowerys.

The pride of character of the Tuscaroras was such that the Cherokees, Creeks, and other tribes joined the whites to subjugate them, and Parkman says that the Tuscaroras were of the same generic stock with the Iroquois and conducted the southern campaigns of those Five Nations.

Hildreth says that they were reputed to be remnants of two Virginia tribes, the Manakins and Manahoas, hereditary enemies of Captain John Smith's Powhatan.

They burned the Surveyor General, who had trespassed on their lands, at the stake, and were in turn partly subjected to slavery by the militia of South Carolina. Eight hundred of them were sold by their Indian enemies to the whites of the Carolinas at one time, and in **1713** most of those at liberty retired through the unsettled portions of Virginia and Pennsylvania to Lake Oneida, New York.

This criminal code, enforced against Allan Lowery, the father of Henry Berry Lowery, the outlaw, has had the result of making Robeson county the seat of a fierce warfare for revenge.

Persons curious about the severity of this code may see a digest of it in Hildreth, Colonial series, vol. II., pp. 271—275.

The Tuscaroras, in their prime, had 1,200 warriors in North Carolina.

In 1807 they bought a tract from the Holland Land Company with the proceeds of their North Carolina lands, and it was about at this period that the ancestor of the Lowerys removed from Halifax county to Robeson county.

THE LOWERYS SETTLE IN ROBESON.

The following statement of the origin of the family is derived from the note-books of Colonel F. M. Wishart, which were entrusted to me to look at by Captain F. H. M. Kenney, of Shoe Heel:—

James Lowery, the grandfather of H. B. Lowery, came from Halifax, N. C., and settled at what is called Harper's Ferry (in the centre of Scuffletown, two miles from Bule's store), built a bridge across Drowning Creek, and kept it as a toll bridge; also kept a public house for the accomodation of travellers.

He was wealthy and fairly respected by all, and owned slaves.

He married a woman by the name of ———, and had three sons, George Travis Lowery, Allen Lowery and Thomas Lowery.

Allen Lowery, the father of the band leader, married a woman by the name of Mary Combes and settled on the south side of Back Swamp, in a desert-looking wilderness, and was the father of Patrick, Purdie, Andrew, Sinclair, William, Thomas, Stephen, Calvin, Henry Berry and Mary.

Old Allen Lowery was a good, peaceable citizen, and well liked.

He was a great hunter in his young days. With his neighbors—Barnes, McNair, Moore and others—he was willing to share his last cent. All his boys were mechanics with him, and the family got on smoothly and industriously until the summer of 1864, when three "Yankee" prisoners escaped among many from the pen at Florence, S. C.

They made their way to the house of Allen Lowery and were comparatively safe, as nearly all the white people were in the Confederate army and the State laws would not allow the mulattoes to enlist in the ranks.

The Scuffletowners were mustered in only as cooks, &c., or conscripted to work on the brestworks about Wilmington.

There is a story current that the Lowerys in the Revolutionary War were tory bush whackers, but it is also alleged that one of the family received a United States pension up to the day he died. Some of the boys were willing to enter the Confederate army; as their father had kept slaves, but their proud spirits recoiled from working on the fortifications among the negroes.

As the war progressed and the Lowerys got to understand it they Sympathized with the North, and entertained at their cabins its escaped soldiery from Florence.

A DEMOCRAT'S ADMISSION.

Mr. Bruce Butler, an earnest democrat and a prominent lawyer in Wilmington, said, in reply to an interrogatory:—

"I don't think politics has anything to do with this outbreak. It began in the war, when our impressing officers made a requisition upon the free negro settlement and pulled away these outlaws or their relatives to work on our fortifications. They complained of the food, the treatment, the work, and so forth, and, I believe, the chief outlaw himself ran away. Then there was hunting made for him and he got to lying out in the woods and swamps; next to stealing, next robbery. Murder and outlawry followed in time—bad begun grew worse —that's my understanding of it."

OLD ALLEN LOWERY

One evening at Lumberton I sat in the office of Judge Leech, half a dozen gentleman present, and they described old Allen Lowery. The disposition generally manifested by the white people of Robeson county is to put little stress upon the murder of this old man, but to ascribe the crimes of Henry Berry Lowery's band to lighter cause and to separate the motive of revenge altogether from his offences.

"The Lowerys," said one of the persons present, "were always savage and predatory. By conducting a sort of swamp or guerilla war during the Revolution they accumulated considerable property, and at the close of that war were landholders, slaveholders and people of the soil. Then they grew dissipated during the time of peace, and their land was levied upon to pay debts. Being Indians, with an idea that their ancestors held all this land in fee simple, they could not understand how it could be taken from them, and for years they looked upon society as having robbed them of their patrimony."

"Yes," said one present, "Allen Lowery brought me a case against a man who wished to sell a piece of property he had formely owned, and he couldn't be made to understand that the man had a good title for it. When they were holding the examination, just before they shot him in 1865 the old man pleaded in extenuation of the plunder found in his house that he had never been given fair play but had been cheated out of his land. He said that his grandfather had been cut across the hand in the Revolution, fighting for the State, and that the State had cheated all his family. He had the Indian sentiment deep in him, of having suffered wrong, and imparted it to all his sons. Here is Sink (Sinclair) Lowery with the same kind of notions to this day. He said a little while ago, 'We used to own all the country round here, but it was taken from us somehow.'"

"He was a good carpenter," said another, "and brought all his boys up in industriously. He built this office in which we sit. He had a peculiar kind of eyes; they would prowl around your face until you got off your guard and then he would give you a piercing look through and through. He had a heap of mixed white and Indian pride, but I believe he was whipped at the whipping post once for pilfering, but that was so far back in his youth that nobody remembered it except by tradition. His son, Sinclair, married a white woman The Lowerys and Oxendines were generally accounted the highest families in Scuffletown."

"Well," chimed in another voice, "he was considerable of a heathen and never went much to church except very late in life, when he became a Methodist class-leader. Old Allen married a girl early in life and had one child, but being indifferent or disappointed about her, he wandered off two years to South Carolina, and when he returned, without divorce or notice of any sort, he married a different woman.

"Taking example from him the first wife also married a new man. By the second wife old Allen Lowery had all these children. Nobody ever had any complaint to make of him or his boys until the murder of Barnes, eight years ago."

THE FIRST MURDER.

Henry Berry Lowery grew up with his father, a carpenter and a hunter.

He was noticed to be a boy of good appearance, quiet address, pleasing and modest enough, but also to cherish deep resentments and to readily take affront. His eyes had hidden in them, and prompt to come forth on provocation, the hazel Indian lights, and when he was ordered to the sand pits, below Wilmington, to do laborer's duty, at the age of seventeen, he ran away, and returned to Scuffletown, where he was repeatedly hunted, and by none more than by John A. Barnes, his father's next neighbor, and by J. A. Brant Harris, a white man of bad character, who domineered over Scuffletown.

He remained for many months between the swamps and the shanties, and was joined by Steve Lowery and other relatives and acquaintances.

Unable to work for a living under these conditions, the party had to forage upon the whites.

Thus, insensibly, formed vagabond and desperate habits, in which, there is reason to believe, they found apt tutors in some escaped Union prisoners who had made their way from Florence, S. C., by the light of the North Star, straight into Scuffletown, and who, to avoid capture, hid in Back and Lumber Swamps with the young Lowerys, Strongs and Oxendines.

Bloody example, the self-reliance of an outcast and distaste for peaceful pursuits soon overcame Henry Berry Lowery, and he grew to hate the slaveholders and to identify himself ideally with the wrongs of all the mulatto settlement.

BRANT HARRIS.

This fellow was a bluff, swaggering, cursing, redfaced bully, entrusted by the rebel county authorities with keeping the peace in Scuffletown and hunting up deserters and conscripts, and he meantime gained a penny by "farming a turpentine orchard," selling rum, &c.

He looked like a slave dealer, and was the terror of the poor wretches of Scuffletown, whom he used to flog, unroof and insult at will.

Being a libidinous wretch he took possession of some of the lightest damsels in the settlement, and one of these was courted honorably by a cousin of young Henry Berry Lowery.

Seeing the white man so much at the hut of his girl one of the young Lowerys threatened among his people to kill Brant Harris if he did not let her alone.

This being reported to Harris he was seized either with apprehension or rage, knowing, perhaps, the Indian qualities of the Lowery lads.

He therefore put himself in ambush to kill the lad who threatened him, but by mistake shot the wrong Lowery, the brother of the boy he hunted.

This mistake made Brant Harris aware that his present peril was greater than before, for he had now raised the savage ire of all the Lowerys and their Indian kin.

He therefore seized both the brothers of his victim as persons who owed military service on the fortifications of Wilmington, and was deputed to march them from Scuffletown to Lumberton.

On the way this monster deliberately murdered both boys, and one of the three, at least, was found with his skull beaten in by a bludgeon.

A fourth brother made his escape to the Lowerys and joined Henry Berry Lowery, who vowed to kill Brant Harris at sight.

The foregoing is thus ingeniously paraphrased by Colonel Wishart in his book said to be designed for publication, part of which, in manuscript, I had the privilege of examining:

"A man by the name of Brant Harris, who had been a sutler and turpentine merchant at Red Banks, had a dispute with the Lowerys (charged to be about stolen chickens) and he finally killed three cousins of Henry Berry Lowery named Jarman, George and Bill."

Now, there is no record that the Lowerys in question were not as respectable as Brant Harris, and it was several years before Henry Berry Lowery's victims amounted to three.

Brant Harris weighed 230 pounds.

His character may be inferred from the fact that some of the females of his surviving family have given birth to mulatto children.

THE MURDER OF BARNES.

Before the fugitives in the woods and kinsmen of the Lowerys had dealt out retribution to Brant Harris the family of Allen Lowery had become embroiled with their nearest neighbor, a bachelor named John A. Barnes. This Barnes was a fine hunter and could track the fugitives with his practised eye through the swamps, so that he was an obstacle to them as well as an enemy.

The following is Captain Wishart's version of this assassination, the first in point of time committed by Lowery's band :—

After the escaped prisoners from Florence reached the Suffletown district they made the acquaintance and sought the hospitality of Allen Lowery's family.

Henry Berry, Stephen and William Lowery, wishing to give their new friends good table fare, went to the neighboring farm of Mr. Barnes, their oldest acquaintance, and stole two of his best hogs, two miles distant, caried them home and salted them nicely away for long consumption.

Barnes followed the cart track to Allen Lowery's house, saw the remains of the butchering and cleaning, and, getting out an officer and a search warrant, swore to his mark on the ears of the hogs, as found on the rejected heads among the offar.

The three young Lowery's—Henry, Steve and Bill—were nowhere to be found.

Barnes requested old man Lowery and all his boys henceforth to keep on his land or he should help to forward them to the batteries to work involuntarily.

Here the struggle commenced and threats passed and repassed.

On the 12th day of December, 1864, while James P. Barnes was going to Clay Valley Post Office, a distance of one mile (the Post Office at the store of Captain W. P. Mores), he was waylaid half way by H. B. Lowery, Bill Lowery and (as supposed or charged) by the Yankees and shot.

He fell with twenty buckshot in his breast and side, and then Henry Berry Lowery deliberately walked up to him with a shotgun, and although Barnes cried, "Don't shoot me again—I am a dying man," the young mulatto Indian, then not more than sixteen or seventeen years of age, replied :

"You are the man who swore to shoot me," and fired another load into his face, shooting off part of the cheek.

The whole party then crept into the swamp and disappeared.

Some of the neighbors, hearing the shooting and hallooing, hurried up and heard the dying statement of Barnes that Henry Berry Lowery was his murderer.

THE FIRST BURGLARY.

Soon afterward these young men went to the house of Widow MacNair, for the purpose of robbing a confederate colonel.

The sick soldier there lent his pistol to the widow, who wounded one of the robbers, and they carried him off to Colonel Drake's, some distance away, and ordered Widow Nash, the only person in the house, to attend to him till well, on pain of death. The man recovered in perfect secrecy.

THE SECOND VICTIM.

It now became Brant Harris' turn.

The young Tuscarora who had taken the first life without a shudder—and that the life of a man generally reputed to be a good neighbor and useful man—built himself a "blind," or curtain of brush and old logs; and as Brant Harris rode by in his buggy, near Bute's store, in the early part of 1865, he was riddled with buckshot,

His horse ran away, and carried him a considerable distance.

Few people sympathized with Harris, although all were now aware of the existence of a savage band of outlaws in the swamps, who resisted and baffled all means to bring them in.

Before any efficient means could be adopted to arrest young Lowery and his brothers and associates in the intricacies of Back Swamp the army of General Sherman, making the grand march, swept on by Cheraw and Rockingham to Fayetteville, and the foragers or "bummers," who strayed out on the flanks, pounced upon Robeson county.

ALLEN LOWERY'S OFFENCE.

At Scuffletown they found in the Lowery's guides, informants and entertainers, who posted them as to the status of the leading rebels of the county, the wealthiest homesteads and such other matters as a rapacious soldiery would wish to know.

Some of the Lowery boys went out with these troops and brought home part of the spoils.

At this period an execution had been levied on old Allen Lowery, and his son Bill, at law, proprietor of the house and ground where the old man and his wife resided. Bill had probably had association with that part of the family which had fled to the swamps, but there is poor testimony that old Allen had ever committed any robberies. His son William, the new master of the place, governed the old man, who was now sixty-five years of age.

DEATH OF THE OUTLAW'S FATHER.

When Sherman's army had passed on to Fayetteville and Raleigh the malignant rage of the people of Robeson county turned upon this old citizen and the helpless part of his family.

They little knew what a young demon they were to arouse for seven ensuing years in the wild boy who resided in the swamps, and whose motto was to be "Blood for blood!"

They resolved that the Lowery's were then committed adherents of the Yankees, that the blood of Barnes and Harris was unaccounted for, and that it was necessary to make an example of somebody in Scuffletown to teach them that the end of slavery was not yet the colored man's triumph.

Blind, inconsiderate, brutal ill-will and cruelty were at the bottom of this movement.

It started between Floral College and what is now called Shoe Heel.

A member of the gang was a Presbyterian preacher named Coble, or Cobill, an old apostle, exhorter and Pharisee of slavery, and one of the leaders in it was Murdoch MacLain, who, six years afterward, tumbled out of his buggy, shot through and through by Henry Berry Lowery.

These, among twenty others, marched upon old Allen Lowery's cabin, and dragged out the old man and his wife, and two of the sons, found on the premises, Sinclair and Bill.

Searching the cabin they found several articles said to have been filched from the white neighbors. This was justification enough.

They carried the old people off to a safe nook and there went through the farce of examining them.

The devil's own priest—Coble or Cobill—got a prayer ready to make at the execution, and to make his holy *role* hypocritically consistent, he pleaded for the life of Sinclair Lowery.

The negroes say these white Ku Klux

made the condemned people of the family dig their own graves.

They stood the old man, at sixty-five years of age, up beside his son, both of them enduring the ordeal with Indian stoicism, and, by the light of blazing torches, as one account relates, shot them to death with duck shot and ball.

Coble or Cobill got off his prayer and perhaps his gun. Before they shot the father and son they endeavored, with blanced fear of the vengeance of the North, to make the poor old wife of Allen Lowery confess to some justification for their act by pointing their pieces at her and firing volleys over her head until she was nearly paralyzed with fear.

From a thicket near at hand Henry Berry, the son of Allen Lowery, saw the volley fired which laid his brother and father bleeding on the ground.

There he swore eternal vengeance against the perpetrators of the act.

Fourteen citizens have paid part of that penalty in the succeeding seven years.

He has been the greatest scourge the South ever knew from one of the inferior race, and has developed a cunning, bloodthirstiness, activity and **courage** unmatched in the history of his race. Some have compared him with Nat Turner.

HENRY BERRY LOWERY AND NAT TURNER.

The insurrection of Nat Turner took place in Southampton county, Virginia, August, 1831, just over the line from Halifax county, North Carolina, where the grandfather of the Lowerys lived.

In Southampton county, as in Halifax, abode Indians, a few of whom still remain—the Nottoways.

Nat Turner was the senior of Henry Berry Lowery, and was thirty-one years of age and a slave.

He was a praying ignoramous and believed himself inspired to kill off the whites, which he commenced, with four disciples, by killing fifty-five men, women and children.

The insurrection lasted only two days and after hiding several weeks the leader was caught and hanged.

Henry Berry Lowery has never been caught and held. He is a bloodthirsty, remoseless, able bandit leader.

In my next letter I shall take up the catalogue of his crimes.

THE BANDIT IN JAIL.

NORTH CAROLINA OSCEOLA.

Further Murders by the Lowery Outlaws. A Comparison. Alive or Dead. High Rewards for the Capture or Killing of the Bandits. Thrilling Stories of the Swamp War. Cold-blooded Assassinations. Sudden Murders, Cool Robberies, Ruthless Retaliation and Footpad Generosity. The Feud with the M'Neills. The Fight. Lowery's Wonderful Escape and Deadly Stratagem. Fearful Death of Sanders, the Spy. Tortured for Three Days, Bruised, Bled, Poisoned, and Finally Shot. Romance Outdone by Facts. How the Success of the Gang Demoralizes Young Scuffletown. The State Powerless.

WILMINGTON, N. C., March 2, 1872.

Since my return and rest in this city I have seen the report of the Ku Klux Committee, which is, in general, confirmatory of the information I have sent you from personal investigation, analysis and belief.

The astounding feature of the Lowery band is that they have so long baffled detection and paralyzed the public spirit and citizen resistance of Carolina. Living upon the border of the North State, they have passed, in their excesses, the boundary line, and some of the murders have been done almost within hearing of South Carolina.

Yet, when the State proposed a vigorous campaign against them, and the militia and volunteers were companies of regular United States troops were finally withdrawn because an equal number of citizens would not operate with them. Adjutant General Gorham stigmatized the militia in a newspaper letter, and said that the regulars, men and officers, obeyed orders and showed cool professional pluck.

This campaign was made at the worst season of the year, the heat and miasma rising and the woods and swamps covered with thick, concealing vegetation.

Twenty-eight volunteers enlisted for this ignominious campaign under Captain Wishart, "the flower of the country," most of them grown to active years since the close of the rebellion.

They were spruce young fellows, fond of a drink and a spree, and I am enabled to present some picture of them from Captain Wishart's diary.

A GLIMPSE OF THE SWAMP WAR.

Thus run four of Wishart's excerpts:—

SATURDAY, August 5.—Militia ordered to Lumberton; a pretty sight! Negroes, mulattoes, whites—all drunk, without arms, ammunition or anything, only money enough to get whiskey.

LATER IN AUGUST.—Two of my men drunk; one lost his boots, one his pistol * * and the pilot was drunk * * The red bugs and yellow flies would kill an elephant * *.

SATURDAY, October 29, 1871.—Henry Berry, Steve, Andrew and Boss were at Bear Swamp Academy to-day at public speaking on educational purposes. All had two double-barrelled shotguns apiece. They captured old J. P. Sinclair, who outlawed them.

LATER IN THE HUNT.—Andrew Strong was seen Saturday, October —, at —, Complained of being nearly worn out.

THE LOWERYS AND THE FLORIDA SEMINOLES.

As there is a cry for United States interference in the Lowery war, it may be timely to advert to a war held in a similar country in the era of Jackson and Van Buren.

THE SEMINOLES

were originally Creeks from Georgia.

They numbered in Florida, 1594 men, and of all sexes and ages 3899, exclusive of 156 negro men, escaped slaves.

To subdue these Seminoles took a campaign of five years and cost $19,500,000, besides the pay of the regular army and losses sustained by settlers from indian ravages.

Above twenty thousand volunteers were called out.

Osceola, the Seminole brave most distinguished, was thirty-two years of age when the war broke out; Nat Turner was thirty-one; Henry Berry Lowery was eighteen.

Osceola was half white, and his English name was Powell, the same with the Florida assassin of Secretary Seward, who was remarked to resemble an Indian when he was hanged as Washington, in 1865.

The Seminoles brought into the field 1,660 Indians and 250 arms-bearing negroes.

Persons familiar with the Florida war trace resemblances between Henry Berry Lowery and the Seminole chief called Coacooche, or Wild Cat.

Both young men, they made war a predatory pastime, grew merry with excitement, were cruelly active, and they both ridiculed and laughed at the soldiery floundering in the mud and water to overtaken them.

...TUDE OF THE CAROLINA NEGROES TOWARD THE OUTLAWS.

In passive allies the Lowerys are nearly as well befriended as the Seminoles, for all Scuffletown wishes them at least no ill.

When the troops pursued the scoundrels they could hear a peculiar bark like that of a cur precede them, and die away in the distance, the mulatto's warning note passed from shanty to shanty to put Lowery on the *qui vive*.

If soldiery or armed men are on the railway train a movement among the negro train hands will be observed as the locomotive approaches the stations of Scuffletown.

What happens in Wilmington to-night will be in the knowledge of the outlaws within fifteen hours.

It is this prescient, omniscient, unaccountable apprehension and intelligence of the Lowery which has stricken the community infested with a dumb terror.

The negroes generally in the State show adherence to these colored murderers.

The Legislature passed a bill, ratified by the Governor February 8, 1872, offering a reward of $10,000 for Henry Berry Lowery, and $5,000 for each of the following men:—Stephen Lowery, Boss Strong, Andrew Strong, George Applewhite and Thomas Lowery.

It was proclaimed as follows:—

Now, therefore, I, Tod R. Caldwell, Governor of the State of North Carolina, by virtue of the authority in me vested by said act above recited, do issue this my proclamation offering the following rewards in addition to those heretofore offered to be paid in currency to the party or parties who shall apprehend and deliver, dead or alive, any of the outlaws hereinafter named to the Sheriff of Robeson county.

This reward, in addition to a small reward offered previously by the State and another by the county, brings the price of the band up to about seventy-five thousand dollars. The attitude of

THE BLACK LEGISLATORS

was ominious. When the question came up of offering an enlarged reward for these outlaws several republicans, chiefly black members, voted against it.

It finally passed by 74 to 18. Cawthorn, colored, and Fletcher, colored, made speeches advocating it.

Mills proposed to increase the reward even more, which Mabson, colored opposed.

Page, colored, offered an amendment to the effect that the reward was to be considered open for thirty days, and meantime the outlaws be permitted to leave the State. This was rejected.

The yeas and nays were called.

The following persons, among others, about half of whom were colored, voted against offering the rewards:—Bryan, Burns, Carson, Hargrove, Heeton, Johnston, Marler, Page, Smith, Reaves and York.

This excerpt shows that Lowery's popularity is not confined to the negroes of Robeson county, but is considerable throughout the State.

He interrupted an educational meeting some time ago with his whole armed band, and demanded the proceedings of the Legislature to be read.

The State Adjutant General, Gorham, stigmatized the Scuffletonians in his report as deceitful and in collusion with the Lowerys.

AFRICAN CHARMS FOR THE BAND.

The superstition of this gang of outlaws has been suggested as a mode of affrighting them.

When Henderson Oxendine was

hanged there were found in his coat pockets a piece of human bone, apparently taken from the human hand, and a quantity of mixed herbs.

Being interrogated as to whether their many bloody deeds had not given the surviving bandits visions of ghosts and fears of being haunted by their dead, the wife of one of them confessed that, although never hesitating in determination, both Henry Berry and Tom Lowery and Andrew Strong were often blue and mentally uneasy.

At this the county newspaper of Robeson—a very complete and sprightly local paper, edited by a clergyman named McDiermid—printed a local about the discovery of spiritual artillery, baneful drugs, witchcraft, &c., intended to be read by the Lowerys, and to fill them with apprehension.

These outlaws take the newspapers daily, and some time ago, in hunting over the deserted shanty of Lowery, a copy of the *Robesonian* was found, with the endorsement torn from the wrapper, and then carrried to the publishing office and the address was there identified.

The person implicated confessed that Henry Berry Lowery gave him the money and ordered him to subscribe vicariously

WHERE DO THEY GET ARMS?

The Lowerys probably procure their improved arms — the breech loaders especially—through some of the more avaricious country merchants, and are made to pay heavy rates with the money they have got by robbery.

They have depleted the whole region round Scuffletown of guns and pistols. In one case a white family slept on their arms and walked with them continually; but one Sunday, releasing vigilance, left their guns for a few moments on the piazza, when the Lowery band, lying in watch, rushed up between them and their arms and drove the men to the woods.

INCIDENTS OF OUTLAWRY.

April 29, 1871. Henry B. Lowery and Boss Strong went to a house in Richmond county and took two mules and a wagon out of a citizen's barn, filled the wagon with corn and drove in style to Scuffletown, where the corn was equally distributed.

Having no use for horses and vehicles they returned the team the same day to the owner.

May 3, 1871, Henry B. and Steve Lowery and Boss and Andrew Strong went on a robbing excursion to the house of Mr. Parnell, near Scuffletown. The males of the family fled to the woods, the females were bolted away in a retired apartment, and the house despoiled.

The bandits waited all night for the males to come home, and threatened to kill them if they inopportunely arrived.

One day in October, 1871, a Mr. McNeill was out in the woods hunting coons with a fine dog which belonged to him.

As the darkness came on he heard what seemed to be human footsteps around the tree he was watching.

Filled with the superstition of Lowery's band he made haste to get home.

Next morning, sure enough, as he sat at Monbeck station, Henry Berry Lowery appeared, armed like a pirate, double-barrelled shot gun, Spencer carbine and five revolvers in his belt, but cool as a cucumber.

He had a dead coon over his shoulder.

"Mr. McNeill," he said, "as your dog treed this coon, I thought it no more than right to bring it to you. I wish you would lend me that dog to coon a little on my own account."

"No," said McNeill, "I can't spare that dog, but I have got another one at home which I might lend you."

"Oh," cried Lowery, "never mind. I guess I can get along without it." And he walked off as demurely as any honest neighbor. To show this outlaw's fearlessness, it may be instanced that when he went to the house of one McKinsley, near Red Bank, he pulled off his whole belt of arms and then threw them down on the piazza while he ordered the family to prepare him a meal in a remote apartment and partook of it there.

The leading white families remaining in Scuffletown are the McNeills, Ed. Smith, Alex. McIntyre, Nick and William Kelly, John McNair, and the Tyners.

The ablest leader against Lowery has been J. Nicholas Maclain, who has been obliged, nevertheless, to leave the county and go to Georgia. He is a light-complexioned man, sallow, wiry, and beardless.

EDITORIAL COURAGE.

Mr. James, local editor of the Wilmington *Journal*, received a letter from a brother editor at Lumberton after the safe robbery in February, 1872, to this effect:—

All the able-bodied men in town have gone west in pursuit of the outlaw. It is needless to say that I start east by the first train.

One Oxendine, commonly called Dick, keeps a bar at Lumberton, unable to have any repose at Scuffletown.

His father was the "best-to-do" negro in that settlement, and was for a time County Commissioner, with a salary of $3 a day.

The Lowerys have not always been a peaceful family, even prior to the war, and it is related that John Quince Lowery killed a relative about 1858, and was branded for it in the hand at Lumberton.

Several of these outlaws have been acquitted before the Courts.

Applewhite was condemned, but broke jail, as did Steve Lowery.

Tom Lowery was in Lumberton jail when Henderson Oxendine was hanged in the jail yard.

Applewhite had been a slave at Goldsboro, and, although a black man, he married a nearly white Oxendine girl.

Andrew Strong married Henry Berry Lowery's sister, if I am correctly informed. Tom Lowery married a girl of Scuffletown named Wilkins, and Steve Lowery married an Oxendine.

THE DEATH OF APPLEWHITE.

It appears to be well established that Applewhite is either dead or laid up from serious wounds received in a combat with the militia, near Red Bank, in October, 1870.

He was fired upon and pursued, and the bloody tracks in the leaves and bushes showed where he had stopped to rest and supper.

His little daughter told the Sheriff and posse that he had been hit in the mouth, neck and breast and could not articulate, and that he repeatedly fainted.

His mulatto wife dressed his wounds with spirits of turpentine, and the miserable man had then to return to the swamp.

Soon after this he was surrounded in Lowery's cabin, and had to escape as best he might by the aid of the band, in the darkness before the dawn.

IN THE SWAMPS.

these outlaws live on little island-like

patches, burrowing under brush, and at one place it was found that they had constructed a commodious cabin.

They seldom move at night except to do robberies, and take advantage of the darkness to slip into the huts of their relatives and befrienders.

LOWERY'S CABIN.

The home of Lowery is now deserted, and its log walls and doors show the marks of bullets, shot and balls fired from the woods and swamps.

There are two doors on the sides, opposite each other, and a trap was at one time concealed in the floor, the hinges hidden or mortised beneath.

This trap afforded admission to a sort of mine or covered way, which ran under the surface about sixty yards to the swamp.

This passage way was filled up several months ago, and the house is no longer tenable by the bandits. Here Lowery was surrounded in May, 1871, by Sheriff MacMillan, George Wisehart and a posse of nine in all, but, after some exchange of shots, Lowery pulled out a small false closet or buttery by the chimney, acting as a concealed door, and he crept off with his entire party.

THE FIGHT AT WIREGRASS LANDING.

A few months later than this, in the autumn season, he performed an escape of almost incredible audacity.

There were twenty-three soldiers at a spot called Wiregrass Landing, and as they looked up the narrow channel of the Lumber River they saw Henry Berry Lowery paddling a small, flat-bottomed scow, his belt of arms unbuckled and thrown in the bottom of the boat.

Instantly the whole party opened fire, when Lowery, with the agility of a terrapin, threw himself into the water on the remote side of the scow, tilted it up like a floating parapet, and reaching inside successfully for his weapons, aimed and fired as coolly as if he were at the head of his band on solid ground.

In this position he actually wounded two of the men and put the whole posse to flight. Sheriff MacMillan vouches for the literal truth of this statement.

A GENERAL JAIL DELIVERY.

Some of the jail breakings of this party have been remarkable.

May 10, 1871, Henry Berry and four other men suddenly appeared in Lumberton jail, where Tom Lowery and Pop Oxendine were heavily ironed.

The rescuers bored with augers around the staples of three doors, and also bored around the irons fastened in the floor, when all the party went forth nonchalantly.

MURDER OF GILES INMAN.

Mr. Inman was needlessly killed while bringing up reinforcements to Sheriff, MacMillan.

Inman was a youth of eighteen or twenty, and a resolute spirit to cleanse the county of its marauders.

The Sheriff of the county had surrounded Henry Berry Lowery's house and had shown the white feather, with a large part of his posse; and therefore, there was a steady cry for the reserves. As in the ballad of Horatio,

Those behind cried, " Forward !"
And those in front cried, " Back."

Lowery, meantime, had secretly and like a snake slipped out of his cabin, and he panted for blood. Throwing himself down in the bushes near the path, only 500 yards from his house where the white hunters lay in force, he ordered his band to pick off the advancing party *seriatim*.

His own carbine brought down Giles Inman instantly.

At the same instant Roderick Thompson, another volunteer, was mortally wounded by Boss Strong, and Frank MacCoy was badly wounded.

Inman's family is said to have been republican in politics.

MURDER OF MURDOCH AND HUGH MACLAIN.

The murder of the two brothers, Murdoch and Hugh MacLain, was achieved while they rode together along the public road in an open buggy, and accomplished after long and cool deliberation.

They had several times approached the dwelling of these young men, and rattled chains and stirred up the domestic fowls and animals, but Murdoch was too prudent to come out.

He was a superb specimen of the self-reliant, impulsive, military Southerner, never capable of acknowledged merit in a negro accompanied with humility, and at the murder of Allen Lowery by the neighborhood he was second in command.

As he was riding along Henry Berry Lowery from a "blind" at the roadside and at close quarters snapped his gun.

Murdoch instantly reached for his arms, which he carried with him perpetually, but before he could bring it to his shoulder he was riddled with buckshot, and the horse started off at a gallop with both brothers mortally wounded.

This murder has been the latest committed by the Lowery band, and its purpose was solely revenge.

In killing MacLain Henry Berry Lowery shed the blood of one of the highest youthful spirits in that region, but one, unfortunately, whose record against the colored race was long and hard and dark.

MURDER OF HECTOR AMD A. T. MACNEILL AND WILLIAM BROWN.

The murders of Hector MacNeill, A. MacMillan and William Brown happened in the summer of 1870, within sight of a large camp of troops and directly upon the railroad track near Bure's station.

It had been deemed sagacious to make prisoner the wife of Henry Berry Lowery and to deposit her and her children in Lumberton Jail as an accomplice of the outlaw chief.

Filled with rage at this act Lowery and his gang made their way rapidly across the swampy country and, throwing themselves down behind some decayed railway tier, waited like panthers for the soldiery to appear.

They came leading the mulatto woman and her children, jocular and unsuspecting.

Suddenly there was a series of reports of firearms, and the three persons named were down on the track moaning in the anguish of mortal wounds.

The woman and children were left standing on the track and the rest of the escort party ran away more or less injured with buckshot.

Berry Barnes was shot in the head and Aleck Brown in the ankle. The troops fired the camp, riddled the woods with ball, but the creatures of the swamp were nowhere to be seen, and the woods resumed their melancholy and silence.

The three victims belonged to the best families of whites in that region, and their summary fate filled the whole country side with the pall of woe and terror.

Society seemed to have become disrupted, the law without avail, and vengeance without call or reach of God or man

I talked on this matter with two of

the intimate white neighbors of the Lowerys—viz., MacNeill, and McLeod. MacNeill is a little, thick-set, aged old man, with hard, twinkling eyes and homespun clothes.

"I think I ought to have some sympathy," he said, "I have been robbed time and again, my wife and daughter shot at my threshold, my son-in-law, Taylor Willard, and his family, returned upon my hands for support, and my sons banished from their country on penalty of death."

"They have robbed me," said McLeod, "of above three thousand dollars, compel me to give them food and set it out on my table for them, and when my wife said the other day to Henry Berry Lowery that he had impoverished us, he answered cooly:—

"Well, I always know where to come when I want anything."

"They took my watch," resumed McLeod, "and stopped me the other day, and seized my pocket-book. Lowery looked over its contents and said, 'Sixteen dollars, is that your whole pile? Well, I won't take that.'"

"I have no desire to see any vengeance done to them," concluded McLeod, "if they only leave the country and never return. I say let them go, for really this band looks like as if it never would be caught and never give us any peace."

THE MURDER OF DANIEL AND MACNEILL M'LEOD.

In Moore county, a night's ride from Scuffletown, a party of disguised men killed Daniel and MacNeill McLeod and stabbed two women and a boy.

The motive was apparently robbery, as the victims were supposed to have been in receipt of a large sum of money, and, as a horse and buggy had been stolen the previous night near Shoe Heel, the act was supposed to have been committed by Lowery's band.

The perpetrators of the act were never discovered, but a negro neighbor of the McLeods was shot dead by the citizens on suspicion of having been a spy of the Lowerys. It is not that clear this band in chargeable with the crime.

The story of John Taylor's death was partly recited in a previous letter, but as a crime, and not merely as a codicil to the death of "Make" Sanderson, it deserves repetition.

THE MURDER OF JOHN TAYLOR.

January 14, 1871, Henry Berry Lowery murdered John Taylor, the most determined and uncompromising of his pursuers, at Moss Neck, on the mill dam, within two hundred yards of soldiers on guard at the railway station.

The outlaws had previously robbed Taylor, threatened him, and sent him word that he should be killed on sight. Taylor had spent the previous night with his father-in-law, William C. McNeill, who lived a short way from the depot.

Saturday morning, at eight o'clock, he started with Malcolm D. MacNeill toward the depot to meet the train. Henry Berry Lowery and two others suddenly rose up from the swamp beside the dam, and Henry Berry fired a shot gun three feet from Taylor's head, sending the whole charge through his head and temples, blowing off part of the skull, and fragments of the brain fell into the mill dam and floated down against the bank with the current.

Steve Lowery almost instantly fired at Malcolm MacNeill.

Henry Berry Lowery ran out of the swamp, seized the quivering body of Taylor by the legs and robbed it of $50 currency.

The troops at the depot rushed down

THE OUTLAW SHOT IN HIS CABIN.

to the spot where the outlaws disappeared into the swamp and fired, and the same evening the Lumberton militia took to the swamps, twenty-five in number, and stayed out all night.

Not finding anything the people began to advocate bloodhounds as the only way of tracking up the desperadoes.

THE MURDER OF JOHN SANDERS.

No crime known to modern society presents such dark, mediæval features as the killing of Sanders, a detective police officer from Boston and a native of Nova Scotia.

It was the concluding portion of a career of wild adventure, and to this day the people of Robeson county turn pale at the bloody reminiscence.

Sanders was one of several man who have sought to obtain the large reward offered for these outlaws, dead or alive, in a sum in gross equal to a handsome little fortune, and he was accredited by the Sheriff of New Hanover county to three or four white republicans of Scuffletown.

Sanders appears to have been destitute of honor; but his scheme of capturing these men was a shrewd one.

Aware that they were anxious to leave the swamps and get safely out of the United States to Mexico, or, at least, to the frontier country, he proposed to show them the way, assume to be their protector and friend, and ultimately to give them up on the road by arranging, beforehand, to have them intersected at some point in South Carolina or Georgia.

At the time Henry Berry Lowery fathomed this design and slew Sanders for his treachery a wagon had been prepared and packed, and the outlaws had fully agreed to slip off, escorting their movables and families under cover of the woods and broken country.

To bind them to his confidence by extraordinary means Sanders prostituted the rites of Masonry and

ORGANIZED MASONIC LODGES

in the Scuffletown region while teaching a small negro school in that vicinity.

He spent eighteen months of persevering cunning to win the sceptical hearts of the bandits, but became himself corrupted by their females, and reckless of speech and association. Being suspected and looked upon with an evil eye for living among the mulattos and teaching them, Sanders also joined the Ku Klux to appease the white population, and, it is rumored, was concerned in several night enterprises, whippings and vigils.

Here we have the perfection of Goblin reality—a man sworn into Masonry and, also, the Invisible Empire, for the purpose of bringing a band of outlaws to justice.

Sanders was a stoop-shouldered, thin-visaged, hook-nosed man, with a broad, sharp forehead; he had keenness of apprehension and undoubted boldness.

He died as he had lived, in mystery, and out of the sight or reach of pitying man, and there is reason to believe that his fate was to be attributed to the want of caution of some of the county authorities who had learned his purposes.

SANDERS' CAPTURE BY THE LOWERYS.

In the middle of December, 1870, Sanders established a camp in a "bay" near Moss Neck, close by the house of William C. MacNeill.

Sanders was a loose talker, and had informed many persons of his object, and MacNiell's sons visited him in his secret camp and gave him advice and information.

According to the statement of one of the MacNeill boys, made before he was warned out of the country, there was a rendezvous of several of the neighbors called at Sanders' camp on Sunday, November 20, 1870. Some of the young men got to the camp at four o'clock in the afternoon, but MacNeill did not arrive until seven o'clock.

As he walked down toward the "bay" the young men slipped up to him and, with ghastly faces, whispered that they were all surrounded and that to move would be certain death, covered, as they all were, by the shot guns and pistols of their besiegers.

The impetuous MacNeill reached his hand toward his pistol, when four men rose up in the bushes close beside him—namely, Henry Berry Lowery, Stephen Lowery, George Applewhite and Boss Strong.

Henry Berry Lowery advanced, with a cool, fiendish look, and took MacNeill's repeater from its case, and told him to make himself at home that night, for he would be detained. MacNeill, disarmed, joined the other prisoners around the outlaw's camp fire.

After dusk Henry Berry Lowery led MacNeill off from the camp into the swamp and said :—

"God damn your soul, I want you to tell me where Sanders is. He is expected here. If you don't tell me where he is and why he don't come I will kill you dead. I intend to kill you anyhow when I get Sanders. You had better own right up!"

Not obtaining anything from MacNeill, the outlaw walked him back to the fire, and, after a little time, Steve Lowery took MacNeill out for a like purpose. Steve Lowery told MacNeill that if he did not make a clean breast of his knowledge of Sanders Henry Berry Lowery would make the whole gang riddle him.

Steve showed MacNeill a pack of cards which he had purchased at the Scotch fair, a few miles from Shoe Heel, and remarked, "We boys go anywhere, and

THE WHOLE COUNTRY BELONGS TO US."

Young MacNeill testifies that all that night messengers were sent out to confer with invisible persons, whose voices were heard on the road side. These posted sentinels and the outlaw leaders in camp kept up communication all night long and toward daylight the bandits grew very impatient and threatened their prisoners many times.

At early dawn Steve Lowery being out on guard, the detained prisoners heard the cry "Halt!" and heard several other voices belonging to persons not seen in the camp. Almost immediately the voice of Sanders, the detective, was heard, saying, "I surrender."

Henry Berry Lowery, George Apple-white, and Henderson Oxendine now ran out and the command was heard to take the prisoner on to the Back Swamp.

In a few moments Henry Berry Lowery and his brother Stephen returned, saying, "We have got the buck we wanted."

Henry Berry Lowery then turned to Malcolm MacNeill and said, "God damn you, I have a great mind to kill you right here. I ought to have killed you before.

"You have been hunting me for years. You are young, stout, and healthy, however, and I don't want to take your blood. I hate to interfere with you and your people; but you have already done so much to have me hanged or shot that it would be right if I should kill you right here. I will let you go this time, however; but you make yourself scarce in this country. Your folks may keep that shebang at Moss Neck; but you won't know when your time has come. Get out of this country mighty quick. Your father may stay here if he wants to, but

TELL HIM TO WALK A CHALK LINE."

Young MacNeill then retired, covered with the rifle of his unappeasable foe, and he lost no time in obeying commands and quitting the country. Sanders, whose voice he recognized, was never seen again by mortal eyes except by the outlaws.

Nearly a month after the arrest of Sanders, and on the testimony of the people detained at his camp by the Lowerys, three persons were arrested as accomplices in the murder and charged with being guardians of the road and entrappers of the unfortunate Sanders.

These were Dick Oxendine, who now keeps a barroom at Lumberton, John Sampson and Robert Ransom.

The end of the unfortunate Sanders was related by Henderson Oxendine, one of the outlaws, prior to his execution, and is fully confirmed by Henry Berry Lowery himself, who said:— "The efficiency and *morale* of my command compelled me to kill Sanders. We all pitied him, but if I hadn't killed him I would have had no right to kill John Taylor or any of the rest."

They marched Sanders to a secret camp on a small island in Back Swamp, near the residence of the late Zach T. Chandler, and proceeded forthwith, with devilish malignity, to torture him, by firing volleys over his head, bruising him with gunstocks and clubs, and finally by administering doses of arsenic to him and

OPENING HIS VEINS WITH A KNIFE.

For three days, or until Thursday, these horrible wretches surrounded their white victim, their dull blue eyes calmly enjoying his agonies, and he reminded every hour that escape or mercy were hopeless.

Human or savage nature, happily, seldom presents a picture so atrocious as one decoyed and disappointed man guarded in the wild swamps of Carolina, but almost within sound of Chrsitian firesides, looking into inevitable and violent death after days of pain.

The victim's fortitude and philosophy earned the respect of his murderers, and before carrying his sentence into execution they permitted him to write a farewell letter to his injured wife and family, which they posted by mail with a sort of grim and military observance of justice.

The object of keeping Sanders alive for the better part of a week has not been explained—whether due to divided councils, love of persecuting him while still alive, or the desire to wrest information from him.

He had reason to lament that he ever left his residence and associations in enlightened New England, to die thus miserably in the swamps of the Pedee region, among the human moccasins that infested it.

On Thursday night the outlaws told Sanders that his time had come, and they blindfolded his eyes and tied him to a tree.

He made a few words of a prayer and gave a signal, and at once Steve Lowery, the darkest Indian of the group,

EMPTIED BOTH BARRELS OF HIS SHOT GUN

into the helpless wretch.

After the hanging of Oxendine, a party of twenty-five soldiers and citizens, led by Mayor Thomas and Lieutenants Horne and Simpson, followed the directions given by Oxendine, and, without difficulty found the camp where Sanders had been confined. It was in the densest part of the swamps, and scattered around were the spade used for digging the grave and some cooking utensils.

They proceeded to search for the remains, and found them decently wrapped in a blanket, and deposited face up, with the hands folded in a dignified manner, and the daugerreotype of

THE MURDERED MAN'S WIFE

reverently placed upon his breast. These cool particularities and deliberation make the tragedy even more heinous by the awe which they inspire.

It is murder with the appearance of sovereignty and martial right.

The occurence will frighten the rising generation of Carolnia for the century to come.

THE ANARCHY CAUSED BY THE LOWERYS.

One looks in vain for any other cause of this fateful and scandalous state of affairs in an old and sedate part of North Carolina than the anomalous fact of a large free negro settlement in a period of slavery, and the shiftless, predatory and insolent dominion of a few families in it of corrupted and savage blood, which could be tamed with difficulty and never quite subjugated.

Freedom fell with almost tropical heat and spontaneity upon this settlement and warmed to active life the Lowery vipers, who proudly essayed to compete in military qualities with the late slaveholders and Confederate soldiery.

Party politics has only availed to intensify, prolong and dignify this strife, while meantime murders reach the score and the robberies are innumerable.

Enough can be said on the side of the Lowerys to give them a trifle of an apology, but the condition of things is now such that all classes of the population are interested in the death and overthrow of these scoundrels, who are worse than Ku Klux—they are Apaches.

They are turning the heads of the colored people and prompting negro imitators, and

THE VERY CHILDREN OF SCUFFLETOWN

are growing up barbarians with the lust for plunder and rapine.

There is little to choose between the politicians of the rival parties.

The undoubted existence of Ku Kluxism—now perished utterly and without mourners or apologists—has made the republicans take the part of the Lowery gang as a necessary reaction and return of resistance.

But the Lowery feud began in 1863, before the Confederacy was suppressed, and proceeded entirely from causes inseparable from the war.

The leader of the gang, and, indeed, all associated with it, have shown a ferocity, a premeditation and an insolence frightful to understand and destructive of all example and order.

The State and county authorities have done their best and accomplished nothing.

The desperation and confidence of the outlaws is greater than ever. They fear nothing and terrify all.

Can Congress or the President permit the colored people of the South to be longer debauched by this spectacle of a few men of color defying a State?

OMINOUS INTELLIGENCE.

Wilmington, N. C., March 23, 1872.

The latest intelligence from the Herald correspondent in the hands of the Robeson county outlaws renders even more grave the question of his probable fate. It was his intention to accompany the outlaws to their several hiding places, they agreeing to carry him to their haunts in the swamp blindfolded, and it was his intention to leave them on Monday next if possible. To-day Rhody Lowery, the wife of Henry Berry Lowery, appeared at the depot at Moss Neck and made a statement to the special messenger of the Herald as to the recent movements of the correspondent.

MRS RHODY BRINGS STRANGE NEWS.

Rhody states that upon the return of the Herald correspondent from Moss Neck yesterday, after his delivery of his package of correspondence for the Herald bureau here, he was seated in her cabin when Andrew Strong and

Steve Lowery suddenly entered and peremptorily ordered him to

"COME AND GO WITH US."

Rhody states the HERALD correspondent, manifesting great trepidation, immediately obeyed their order, and was last seen by her moving in company with the outlaws, whose manner toward him was sullen and menacing, in the direction of the swamp. Rhody has seen nothing of the HERALD correspondent since his departure from her cabin, and she professes entire igorance of the disposition made of him by the outlaws.

AN OMINOUS HINT.

In connection with this I make an extract from a letter from your correspondent of yesterday. He says:—"In a conversation with Andrew Strong and Steve Lowery of yesterday I asked if I could see 'Boss,' who they say is not dead, though I know he is, and Steve, with a laugh, said to Andrew, 'Yes, he shall see Boss before he goes away,' which remark was accompanied by a villanous chuckle. I am on parole now. They made me put my hand on my heart and swear I would not try to run away, and then I gave them full permission to kill me if I did, and not accuse them at the Day of Judgment. They treat me well, except that they compel me to drink their infernal whiskey."

Rhody Lowery's statement concerning the HERALD correspondent, taken in connection with the ominous utterances of Steve Lowery, has created a feeling of profound apprehension here regarding his fate.

———

THRILLING FACTS.
———

The Herald Correspondent Among the Lowery Bandits. A Week in the Hands of the Lowerys. The Father of the Oxendines. The Mother of the Lowerys. Her Bitter Story by the Grave of the Murdered. Rhody Lowery, the Queen of Scuffletown. Face to Face With the Terrors. Their Appearance and Equipment. A Night in Rhody Lowery's Cabin. Life of the Hunted men.
  Terrible Tales From Terrible Tongues. A Blindfold Journey to Their Hiding Places—The Island Armory. Released from Bondage. Excitement in Wilmington.

WILMINGTON, N. C., March 25, 1872·

ARRIVAL OF THE CORRESPONDENT.

To the amazement, and yet to the great satisfaction, of the public here the HERALD correspondent who has been for nearly ten days past in the swamps of the Carolina outlaws returned to Wilmington this afternoon by the Charlotte road, which traverses the Scuffletown district. Up to the time of his arrival in Wilmington little or no hope was indulged of his safety, in view of the threats against him which have recently been made by the outlaws. His safe arrival in Wilmington this afternoon

CREATED AN INTENSE EXCITEMENT,

and despite the fearfully stormy weather the HERALD correspondent was the object of curiosity and the HERALD was the theme of discussion and praise. The universal sentiment in Wilmington is that the HERALD correspondent is the hero of a wonderful feat of daring, and there is universal rejoicing that he has finally escaped the great perils which have for more than a week past environed him. Details given by your correspondent regarding his adventures among the outlaws confirm the accounts given in the HERALD despatches of the

PERIL AND DIFFICULTIES

which he has undergone. He left for New York this afternoon, and will give to the HERALD the fullest possible details of his thrilling adventures. On Friday last your correspondent was taken by the outlaws farther into the swamp, and

CONDUCTED BY THEM BLINDFOLDED

from Rhody Lowery's cabin to several of their most secret hiding places. At the moment of leaving Rhody's cabin the HERALD correspondent experienced the greatest sense of personal danger suffered by him during his career with the outlaws. Tom Lowery had especially urged the killing of the

"DAMNED YANKEE,"

and as the other outlaws conducted him away from Rhody's cabin, with the remark to Rhody that he would never see daylight again, your correspondent had little hope but that Tom Lowery's savage threat would be executed. Conducted by outlaws through the swamp blindfolded, except when his captors chose to remove the bandage, he traversed the swamp, in some places wading almost

WAIST DEEP IN WATER,

and again reaching solid ground, thus gaining one of the hiding places of the outlaws, which he inferred to be situated upon an island. The blindfold was removed, and he found himself an inmate of a low, pitched cabin, in which a moderately tall man could not possibly stand erect. In this cabin were from

THIRTY TO FORTY SHOT GUNS

but no smaller arms. The outlaws would not permit him to look out of the window and make any observations of the surroundings. He was told that he was already the possessor of more of their secrets

THAN ANY OTHER HUMAN BEING

outside of their gang, and more than they intended anybody else should ever have access to again. While in the swamps your correspondent was repeatedly informed by the outlaws of their suspicions that he would attempt to chloroform them, and that he was a government spy sent to repeat the *role* in which the Detective Sanders had been caught by them.

A DEMOCRATIC DEMON.

He was also told by Steve Lowery that a prominent democrat of Robeson county had given them information that he was a federal spy and that he would undoubtedly do them great harm before he left them.

"Still," said Steve, " we believe that you are honest, and we will trust you; but

DON'T UNDERTAKE TO COME HERE AGAIN

because you know too many of our secrets." Steve then added, " We have trusted three other men besides you and they all betrayed us, but still we will trust you and let you

GIVE THE HERALD ALL THE INFORMATION

you can about us." After leaving the swamps the outlaws carried your correspondent on Sunday back to Rhody's cabin, and this morning accompanied him to Moss Neck,

WAVING A FRIENDLY ADIEU TO HIM

as the train left. As a mark of their confidence in the honesty of his intentions toward themselves, the outlaws gave the HERALD correspondent

A DOUBLE-BARRELLED SHOT GUN, formerly belonging to Henry Berry Lowery, the deceased outlaw chief, and Steve Lowery presented him with three silver pieces, to be given, one to his wife, another to his baby, and the third to be kept by himself as a souvenir of his trip among the Carolina outlaws. Your correspondent is warm in his acknowledgment of Rhody's services to himself in aiding him to retain the confidence of the outlaws, and.

PRAISES HER COURAGE

and intelligence. Rhody carried him to many points of interest, among others to the grave of the unfortunate Sanders, a spot which the outlaws seemed to dread visiting with a remakable superstitious apprehension. Upon one occasion the HERALD correspondent was within half a mile of the grave of Sanders and begged the outlaws to

CONDUCT HIM TO THE GRAVE,

but they refused, as they also did to visit the graves of other victims of their vengeance.

The satisfaction of the community of Wilmington at the safe arrival in their midst of the daring Herald correspondent is heightened by his confirmation of the previous tidings from him of the deaths of Henry Berry Lowery and of Boss Strong, the second in cleverness and courage of the gang of outlaws. During the absence of your correspondent in the swamps the excitement in Wilmington was at fever heat and found some curious forms of expression.

FIRST LETTER FROM OUR CAPTURED CORRESPONDENT.

SCUFFLETOWN, ROBESON COUNTY, N. C., MARCH 1, 1872

That the thrilling pictures given in the Herald of the outlaws of the Robeson county swamps, in North Carolina, with the history of their deeds of daring murder and rapine, had awakened a deep sensation over the United States, was everywhere evident. It seemed incredible that a band of five men should persistently defy a community such as the Old North State. The criminal supineness of the State authorities, the inactivity of the federal government and the terrorized condition of the inhabitants of the district all expressed an anomalous condition of affairs which

CALLED FOR THE FULLEST INVESTIGATION.

The account given by another correspondent had exhausted all the information surrounding the gang, had given graphic sketches of the now famous mulatto settlement, with its ominous name of Scuffletown, had detailed the outrages by the gang, and traced back their history to the days of the rebel fortifications at Wilmington, when Henry Berry Lowery first took to the swamps, to avoid impressment to work with the slaves of the Southern planters. Escaped federal prisoners, too, from the Confederate prison at Florence. S. C., were seen flitting across the swamps and

HIDING FURTIVELY AMONG THE SHANTIES

of the free negro settlement of Scuffletown to take their places awhile with Henry Lowery and his fellows in the swamps. By and by came the sweep of Sherman's army to the sea, and it was related how the "bummers" found guides and supporters among the free mulattoes of Scuffletown.

It came out, too, in a ghastly way, that the rebel whites of the district, wishing to wreak their vengeance on the colored people, came in the night to old Allen Lowery's cabin, and, dragging forth himself and his son William, mercilessly

SHOT THEM, FATHER AND BOY,

with the one volley, and then went their way, putting two of their supposed enemies out of the way only to create a pack of avenging devils in the persons of the old man's sons and their outlawed friends.

The war closed, and, rightly or wrongly, the white people of Robeson county true to their murder of the father, exempted the Lowerys from the act of oblivion. How truly has it been said that "we can never forgive those we have injured!"

The end of the strife between North and South brought no peace to Scuffletown The "angels" were in the swamps robbing by day murdering by night; the rebels had become Ku Klux, and from fighting manfully in the sunlight were trooping in

THEIR MURDEROUS MASQUERADE,

under the pines and cypresses at night and dragging a negro here and there from his shanty, let him sing his wild, hurried prayers for a minute or two, and then stopping it all with buckshot, but carefully skirting the outlaws themselves, some day to fall, like John Taylor, under a "bead" drawn by Henry Berry or one of his brother outlaws.

This was not civilization. The irresponsible *lex talionis* of the hater and hated, the state of things that created in the land of Muscovy between serf and feudal master the phrase that described the murder of the latter by the former as "the wild justice of revenge," existed in the land of the Lowerys with more degrading surroundings than ever before or in any other country.

That social, restraining force called government had failed to put an end to it, and there seemed, previous to the HERALD's *expose*, to be a sort of *laissez aller* agreed on in tacit apathy by all parties.

But even yet the outlaws themselves had not spoken.

THE OUTLAWS STORY FOR HIMSELF

was unuttered, except through his sentence of death by word of mouth, followed pretty surely by execution through the barrel of a rifle.

In perhaps any other state of things no more would be needed previous to setting about his censure. As things stood it seemed that there must be something needing fuller detail—something of moment in their position which neither the shivering sympathizers of their own race nor the vaunting but trembling white foes thereof would or could impart. This was to be got from the outlaw's lips along.

It did not require much deep reasoning to arrive at this conclusion. It forced itself naturally forward, and the journal which had enterprise enough to gather the first part of the story could surely learn the second.

Without, then, any feeling of rashness or bravado that I am aware of, but simply in the exercise of a grave duty, to shrink from which would be abhorrent to my nature,

I LEFT FOR THE WOODS AND SWAMPS

of Robeson.

My preparations were simple as my mission was direct, and relying on my ability to make the honorable nature of my purpose apparent even to the desperate men it was my deliberate purpose to meet face to face.

Passing over the incidents which do not properly belong to my narrative, I may say that on my arrival in Wilmington I found the Lowerys and the HERALD *expose* to be the only topics of interest in that quiet Carolina town, and the tone of the well-dressed, lounging chivalry about the hotels was not at all encouraging.

I told the object of my visit to several, and the universal verdict was

"A DANGEROUS GAME, STRANGER,

rather you than me." They recalled to me with all the discouraging emphasis which a slow ejaculation of alternate words and tobacco-spittle can command the fearful fate of Saunders, the detective, and generally finished by saying:—

"AN' HE WAS SMARTEHR'N YOU LOOK, STRANGER."

This continual replication of warning did not tend to cheer me.

It recalled in a painful way I had never before imagined the poem of Excelsior with its dismal forebodings of a fatal ending to my venture, but I dashed these all away. The thought that Longfellow's aimless young madman who died in the snow, had nothing in common with a man endeavoring in his own humble way to serve the civilization which lay so sadly wrecked out in the swamp region beyond.

If the scare had reached Wilmington, I reasoned, I shall not then have much difficulty in getting the whites of Robeson county to assist me in ridding them of the objects of their terror through, perhaps,

A MORE MERCIFUL WAY

than killing them off like dogs. But in this I was destined to be mistaken

Excepting Captain Morrison; the "king of conductors" on the Wilmington, Charlotte and Rutherford Railroad, and Ed Hayes, of Shoe Heel, no one encouraged me to proceed.

From the ticket agent, from whom I bought a ticket for Moss Neck, at Wilmington, with his horrified ejaculation—

"My God! stranger, you are not going to stop there!"

To the merchants of Shoe Heel, who assured me death would be the sure fate of any stranger who would venture into Scuffletown, I heard but the one opinion, that the Lowerys were devils and would welcome an opportunity to kill a white man.

Before leaving Wilmington I prepared

A LETTER, DIRECTED TO H. B. LOWERY,

stating that I desired to interview him for the HERALD and offered to give myself into his hands if we would grant me the interview.

It was my intention to stop at Moss Neck and attempt to find a messenger who would deliver my letter, but on the train Captain Morrison advised me to go on to Shoe Heel where I would find better accomodations than at Moss Neck, and from where I could certainly send a messenger to the outlaws.

I took his advice, but was unable to find any one in or about Shoe Heel who would deliver or who knew any one who would present my petition to the "King" of Robeson county.

The reported killing of Boss Strong, it was supposed, had

SO ENRAGED THE OUTLAWS

that the time was particularly inauspicious for my visit.

I met here James McQueen, or Donahoe, of Richmond county, N. C., who asserted he had killed the notorious Boss.

He is a tall, awkward, shambling,

dark complexioned man, of Scottish decent, twenty-five years of age; he has very small eyes, which he has a trick of dropping the instant he is looked at.

The next morning, March 14, I left Shoe Heel and came to Eureka, or Buie's Store, half way between Moss Neck and Red Bank.

At the store, close to the railroad, the colored clerk, of whom I enquired the road to Patrick Lowery's, left the store to point it out to me.

To him I stated the object of my visit, and asked him to inform any of the outlaws he might see what I was after.

THE FATHER OF TWO MURDERERS.

Soon after leaving the store I met an old negro who asked me if I was looking for anybody, when I told him I wanted to go to Pat Lowery's. He told me I was in the right road, and added:—

"I's skeered of strangers most to deff, but you hain't got no gun."

This was Jack Oxendine, the father of Henderson, who was hung in Lumberton in 1870, and Calvin, who is now in the Wilmington jail, charged with being implicated in the King murder.

At the conclusion of his introduction he said:—

"'Fore God, dis is powerful bad country to live in; ebery now and den de Ku Kluck come in yer, and with their shootin' an' whippin' an' hangin', an' de men out by deyselves totin' dere guns, I's scart to deff."

A short half mile from the station brought me to

THE HOME OF PAT LOWERY,

the oldest brother of Henry Berry, and a preacher. When I got there he was working in his carpenter shop, near his house—for he is not above honest labor notwithstanding his profession. I at once unfolded the object of my calling, and asked if I could be permitted to stay with him a few days while I would make efforts to meet the outlaws. He was perfectly willing I should make his house my home while here, but thought my chance of seeing Henry was very slim.

It had been reported for the past four weeks that he was dead, and many believed it, even some of his friends, while the majority thought the story had been originated by his wife and brothers to cover his escape from the county.

Patrick told me Steve and Tom Lowery

HAD PASSED HIS HOUSE A FEW DAYS BEFORE,

but it might be a long time before they would be in their immediate neighborhood again.

After a long conversation between him and James Oxendine, a well-to-do mulatto farmer living near by, it was decided that my best plan would be to go over to the home of old Mrs. Lowery, the mother of Patrick and Henry.

They both assured me it would be perfectly safe, for the outlaws never interfered with any but those who troubled them.

For a consideration Patrick consented to give me his horse on which to ride over, and his son Allen, a bright boy of sixteen, to guide me. After a dinner of

CORN BREAD, BACON AND COFFEE,

we started on our journey, and I must confess to a slight sinking of the heart as I lost sight of the railroad and plunged into the swamps, the lurking places of the Lowery outlaws.

IN THE OUTLAW'S LAND.

I had ridden about a mile, when the discomfort produced by my horse's miserable gait, and the banging of my valise against my legs, became too great, and I proposed to my guide that he should ride awhile.

But the change was not for the better, and it had scarcely been made when we came to one of the low places in the road that are so common here, called " branches," and which are feeders to the swamps

Along one side of these branches are laid, or erected on stumps, logs for the convenience of pedestrians.

They are generally unhewn, all very narrow, many of them decayed, and very few that stand firm under any movement. At the first of these I came to, after dismounting,

I LOST MY BALANCE,

and got into the water knee deep. I remounted the horse, then, and, excepting the gait and banging aforesaid and crushing of my legs against the trees, first on one side and then on the other, as I followed Allen in the narrow footpath through which he led me, I suffered no great inconvenience.

About two and a half miles from Patsedo we came to the " Back Swamp," where for about three hundred and fifty yards the black water crosses the road flowing sluggishly through the brush, and cypress trees.

Along the foot logs here Allen ran, with the confidence inspired by long practice.

ANDREW STRONG'S CABIN.

About a mile from the Back Swamp we passed the cabin of Andrew Strong, one of the outlaws, where his younger brother, Boss, was shot the Friday before.

We passed close to the house, and a couple of women came to the door, and stood there as long as the house was in sight.

As I have since learned, there was another pair of eyes watching us from a thicket near the house. Andrew Strong himself, with

HIS GUN READY FOR A SHOT,

in his hand, studied me as I passed. Another long stretch of water, mud, and sand, and we came to Henry Berry Lowery's house, now in the occupancy of his wife, Rhody. A quarter of a mile further and we reached our destination, the home of

OLD MRS. ALLEN LOWERY.

Here we were greeted by the loud and decidedly savage barking of three large dogs. Two or three very light mulatto girls drove them away, and opened the gate for me; as I passed in I was put in the presence of the old woman, who gave me a very hospitable reception, and assured me I was welcome to stay as long as I pleased, if I could put up with their rough fare.

Mrs. Lowery has the largest house in this section of country; it is weatherboarded, has four good sized rooms, and a kitchen attached, and a wide porch in front. It is on a plantation containing about seventy-five acres, and has numerous out-buildings connected with it. There has been no division of the estate or property since old Allen Lowery was killed, the children

GIVING ALL THE PROFITS TO THEIR MOTHER.

One son, Sinclair, living near, superintends the farm, and assists her when necessary. This little plantation produced last year eight bales of cotton and four hundred bushels of corn.

Soon after my arrival I met Sinclair, who is a dark mulatto, with a good

BOSS STRONG ON GUARD.

countenance. He told me he did not know whether Henry Berry was alive or dead; that no one had seen him for four or five weeks. Mrs. Lowery said the same. Sinclair added:—

"I will be glad if he is dead, for he is a very bad man, and has done a heap of harm."

He further told me he had not been on friendly terms with Henry since the marriage of the latter to Rhody Strong; the marriage it had been announced would be solemnized at his mother's house, and Sinclair, fearing that an attack would be made on the house by the officers in pursuit of Henry, objected to the ceremony being performed there. When Henry was arrested he accused Sinclair of having informed on him, and they had never been on good terms afterwards. Steve and Tom

TOOK PART WITH HENRY

in his quarrel; so that Sinclair could give me no information of the outlaws.

I would here remark that this band are known in their neighborhood by the name "outlaws;" their friends call them and they style themselves outlaws.

When I returned to the house after the conversation with Sinclair, who was working in a field. I was presented to Rhody, the wife of Henry Berry Lowery.

THE "QUEEN OF SCUFFLETOWN."

This young woman is remarkably

pretty; her face oval, of a very light color; large, dark, mournful-looking eyes, with long lashes; well shaped mouth; with small, even teeth, well rounded chin; nose slightly *retrousee*, with profusion of straight jet black hair, combine to make her a very pleasant object to gaze at. She has small hands and feet, and on the latter she wears No. 2, and still cramps her feet less than the majority of white women. She is of medium height, with a very well developed figure, and is between twenty-one and twenty-two years old. When I add that she has a low sweet voice, and a great many little graceful motions of her head and body, it will be seen that she is a *rara avis* in Scuffletown. To the above description I regret that I am compelled to add that this queen cannot write, that

SHE SMOKES A PIPE AND RUBS SNUFF.

When Rhody learned the object of my visit she said she would undertake to have my message conveyed to the outlaws, and she had no doubt they would grant me an interview. Henry Berry, she said, was away, and she could not tell when he would return. I walked home with her, and examined carefully the home of the notorious outlaw leader.

THE OUTLAW'S NEST.

The cabin of this man is built precisely as are all those of the poorer mulattoes—one story high, logs from three to eight inches apart, the interstices not filled in as in log houses at the North, but covered by boards on either the inside or outside, never both. This house had the boards on the outside. There are two doors, opposite each other, secured by modern bolts and buttons, and on the third side is the capacious hearth or fireplace, with chimney built of logs, lined and floored with clay. On the side opposite the fireplace stands the bed, and above and beside it are stretched several poles, upon which hang the clothes of the family.

There are no windows, nor any openings for light but the doors and chimney. Indeed, of some twenty houses of mulattoes I visited, I found but two, those of Mrs. Allen Lowery and Patrick Lowery, in which there were windows.

The house of H. B. Lowery is within a small enclosure, which is surrounded by a large one, and is on his father Allen's estate. The furniture of this house consists of

A BED, A TABLE, THREE CHAIRS,

and three stools. Over the fireplace are pasted a number of pictures cut from the illustrated papers, while a colored print, labelled "The Two Beauties," hangs over the table. Rhody had left her "help"—a light mulatto, who had been engaged by Andrew Strong to stay with her for six weeks for a pair of shoes and a calico dress—in charge of

HER CHILDREN—

Sally Ann, aged five; Henry Delany, aged three, and Neelyann, aged one year and two months. They are all of a very bright color, strong, active, and healthy, the boy being particularly bright. He is said to bear a strong resemblance to his father.

I spent an hour or more with Rhody. She told me, further, if I would come back the next morning she might have some information for me, and that in the meantime I might rest assured I would be in no danger from the outlaws or their friends.

BY THE OLD MAN'S GRAVE—OLD MRS. LOWERY'S STORY.

The next morning (March 15) old Mrs. Lowery took me to a small unenclosed grave in a field near her house, where, marked by four rails lying on the ground, was the grave of her husband and son William. The old woman's voice was broken, and the tears rolled down her withered face even now as she told me how they met their death.

There had been no trouble between them and any of their white neighbors, except that some of their sons had fled from the officers who wanted to take them to work in the rebel fortifications at Wilmington.

In 1864 a party of whites, commanded by James Barnes, came to the house and took the old man and William away, at the same time,

THEY ASKED FOR SPADES,

and took some along with them; some of them returned directly and carried old Mrs. Lowery and her two daughters to the house of a white man, Robert McKensie, where they were locked up in a smoke house.

Mckensie then went away saying he was going up to see how the Lowery men were faring.

When they returned home, in a thicket not far from the house, they found a new-made, shallow grave, in which were the bodies of Allen and William Lowery, lying one above the other, riddled with musket balls.

The next day they came back and took me out into the woods and said they were going to kill me if I didn't tell them where the Yankee prisoners were hid. I didn't know and I told them so, but they wouldn't believe me. They blindfolded me and tied me to a tree, and said they were going to shoot me. I heard them firing, and then I fainted. When I fainted they untied me and sent the girls to bring me too.

This was old Mrs. Lowery's story, and all the mulattoes whom I met and questioned about it, told me about the same thing.

From the grave of the Lowery's I went straight to Rhody's house. As I entered the gate of the outer enclosure I noticed a man standing in the doorway who stepped back within the house. As I reached the inner gate he again came to the door and

I CONFESS TO SOME NERVOUSNESS

as I saw his equipments. But it was no time to stop now, and in a moment I was in Henry Berry Lowery's house, in the presence of Steve Lowery and Andrew Strong, two of the famous swamp outlaws. With as composed an air as the nature of the case would permit I stepped forward.

"I believe these are the men" (I am not sure but that I said gentlemen) "I wanted to see," and extended my hand to the one nearest me, who grasped it cordially as Rhody mentioned his name, Andrew Strong, and mine, and then repeated the ceremony with Steve. Both of them offered me chairs; but I accepted that from which Andrew had just arisen, it being nearer the fire, and immediately

EXPLAINED MY PURPOSE

in seeking them. I told them the great paper of America had given some attention to them, and had published their histories as furnished by the white people of Robeson county; but that the people of the United States might have a clear and just conception of affairs here I had been sent down to see them, hear their stories and the circumstances that had made them outlaws and see now they lived. I told them further that

I HAD NO WEAPON BUT A SMALL REVOLVER,

which they could have while I was with them, but which they would oblige me by returning when I left them.

They replied that Rhody had told them the nature of my business, that they were glad of an opportunity of giving their story to the country, for the "papers were telling so many d—d lies about them," that I would be perfectly safe with them, and that I might keep my pistol.

THE MEN I MET.

Steve Lowery is five feet ten inches high, thick set, with long arms and legs, and is very strong; he has a very dark yellow complexion, hazel eyes, bright and restless, black straight hair and thin mustache and goatee. He was armed with a Spencer rifle, two double-barrelled shot guns, one of the latter and the rifle being slung from his shoulders, and three six-barrelled revolvers in his belt, while two United States cartridge boxes hung from his shoulders.

Andrew Strong is nearly white, about six feet high, with rather mild eyes and reddish beard and hair, the latter cut short. He carried a heavy rifle and the same number of shot-guns, revolvers and cartridge boxes as Steve Lowery, besides a heavy canvas haversack. His *impedimenta* ("turn," he calls it) weighs not less than a hundred pounds. He

ADJUSTED ALL HIS EQUIPMENTS ON ME,

and I could barely stagger across the floor with them. After a few general remarks, Andrew told me they would tell me all I wanted to know if I would question them.

As the shooting of Boss was the chief topic I had heard discussed after leaving Wilmington, I told them I had seen James McQueen or Donahoe, at Shoe Heel, and had taken down his version of the affair, and would now like to know if it was correct. I read to them McQueen's story as follows:—

DONAHOE'S STORY OF KILLING BOSS STRONG.

"Last Thursday night (May 7), I reached the house of Andrew Strong, on the edge of Scuffletown, about ten miles from here, at twelve o'clock, I fixed a good blind about 150 yards from the house, and lying down, I watched the rest of the night and all the next day, eating some provisions I had brought along. About half-past seven P. M. Friday, Andrew came out of the woods, and after stopping and looking around him in all directions he went into the house, and directly come out and gave a low call, when Boss came out of the woods to the house; they were each armed with two rifles and two or three revolvers. A little after eight o'clock, when I thought they would be at supper, I slipped up to the house and looked in through the cat hole in the door, as I supposed they were eating their supper by the light on the hearth. Beside Andrew's wife, Flora and a Miss Cummings were there. I kept watching there until Boss laid down on the floor with his feet to the fire and his head towards me and commenced

PLAYING ON A MOUTH ORGAN.

Then I saw my chance, and I pushed the muzzle of my rifle (a Henry) through the cat hole until it was not over three feet from his head, took a steady aim by the light of the fire and shot. When I fired the women screamed and said:—

LIKENESS OF SANDERS THE SPY.

"HE'S SHOT," "NO HE ISN'T," "YES HE IS," and I looked in as quick as I could get my gun out of the way. Boss' arms and legs had fallen straight from his body, and there was a little movement of the shoulders as if he was trying to get up. Andrew Strong was then standing

IN THE SHADOW IN THE CORNER

and he stayed there until I left. He said to his wife, "Honey, you go out and see what it is," and opened the door opposite the one I was at and pushed her out, but did not come around to the side I was; but went in directly and said there was nobody about. He sent her out again, telling her to look in the corners and jams; but before she had got well out, he said, "Come back, Honey, he was blowing on that thing and it busted and blowed his head off," and directly after he said, "My God! he's shot in the head; it must have come from the cat hole," and sent his wife out again, and I slipped off. When I returned the cat hole was shut up and the house was all dark. Then I come back to Shoe Heel."

THE OUTLAWS HOLD A COUNCIL.

Before they left they went out of the house and held an animated conversation of perhaps half an hour's duration in the garden, after which Steve addressed me:—

"We've trusted three men before and ebery one of dem betrayed us, an' we swo' we'd neber trust no stranger agin, but you look honest, an your story 'pears to be all right, an' we is gwine to trust you some. Now you's got about Donahoe's shootin Boss, we are gwine to keep you heah till you can

PUT IN DE PAPER HOW WE KILLED DONAHOE.

We won't hurt you, an' you kin travel about whar you hab a mind to in dis place, but you must swear an oath dat you won't try to go away without us lettin' you".

I was somewhat dismayed at this speech, but expressed myself satisfied with the arrangement. I saw I would have an opportunity of seeing wild life not often enjoyed by Northern men, and felt that I was in no great danger if I acted honestly towards my captors.

PART TO MEET AGAIN.

The outlaws then slung on their equipments, and after promising to meet me at the "New Bridge," three miles distant, the next morning, strode into the heavy pine forest, and I went back into the cabin, where Rhody taught me how to rub snuff.

Scuffeltown, March 22, 1872.

THE DEATH OF HENRY BERRY LOWERY.

As this letter cannot be read by the people of this settlement before I have left it, the most important piece of information I have to communicate shall be given first. Henry Berry Lowery, the notable chief of the notorious swamp outlaws is actually dead. This is denied by all of his comrades, and his relatives profess to be ignorant of his fate. But from evidence the most reliable, when connected with a well-connected chain of circumstances, I am enabled to give you a correct account of

THE DEATH OF THIS ROBBER CHIEF.

Between February 13 and 16, in company with his *fidus Achates*, Boss Strong, Henry Berry Lowery was ranging the country in the neighborhood of Moss Neck in search of some persons whom he had been informed were hunting him, while Steve and Tom Lowery and Andrew Strong were stationed at a rendezvous on Lumber River, near the "new bridge." About one and three-quarter miles from Moss Neck station, within short gunshot of the road leading from Inman's Bridge to McNeill's mill, they discovered in the bushes a newly made "blind" (a place of concealment or ambush made by intertwining the branching of the thickly grown bushes.)

It was not then occupied, and Henry Berry, believing it had been recently made by one of his pursuers, who would shortly return to it, ensconced himself in it, while Boss made a blind for himself a short distance off, covering the road. But a few minutes after they had placed themselves in their respective positions the report of a gun was heard from Henry's hiding place, and when Boss, who waited to hear a word from his chief or an answering shot from an enemy, cautiously approached the spot, Henry Berry Lowery lay on his back, with one barrel of his shotgun discharged and his nose, forehead and the

WHOLE FRONT OF HIS HEAD BLOWN OFF.

The broken ramrod and the missing wiper showed he had been trying to draw a load from his gun. Boss drew the body into a thicket, and notified his companions, who straightway buried him where, in all human probability, the eye of man will see him never.

Thus perished this remarkable man, and his death marks the dissolution of this most formidable body of desperadoes. The large sum of money he was said to be in posession of is also lost to the country, for no member of the band, not even Boss nor his wife, knew the whereabouts of his treasure chest. The remaining outlaws have made diligent search, but as yet have had their labor for their pains. Henry Berry was said to have had a good deal of money, besides his share of the proceeds of the Lumberton Bank, from which some thirty thousand dollars were taken. It appears to have been his habit of appropriating to his own use

THE LION'S SHARE OF ALL MONEY

taken, giving the subjects the other booty.

But to resume the story of my life among the outlaws. A little after dark on the evening of the day I met Andrew Strong and Steve Lowery I returned to Henry Berry's house, in pursuance of his wife's invitation, to spend the night there.

After supper Rhody said

I SHOULD SLEEP IN THE BED,

while she would make a couch for herself, help and family on the floor.

The next morning, after a breakfast on the same chicken we had tried the night before, with a guide furnished by the friends of the outlaws, I started on horseback for the New Bridge. On the way I passed the "Devil's Den," a desolate wild spot in the Back Swamp, where is said to be one of the hiding places of the bandits.

Our destination was Moss Neck, where I wanted to mail some letters and send some private despatches to the telegraph office at Wilmington, and they wanted to

SEND THEIR MESSAGE TO THE HERALD.

We heard the train east coming when we were about a mile from the station, and ran the whole distance from there. They would not go up to the train, nor would they let me go until I promised them solemnly, with my hand on my heart, that I would not go off in it, and would hand their despatch, as well as my own, to the conductor.

From Moss Neck, with a young man who had been taken prisoner by the outlaws, when they captured the detective Saunders, but who now appeared to be on very good terms with them, we went down the railroad about a mile and then half a mile south into a "bay," where Saunder's "camp" had been located.

From this desolate spot we returned to Moss Neck, where

I MET THOMAS LOWERY,

another of the outlaws, and upon whose head is set a price of $5,000. Tom Lowery is five feet ten inches high, strongly built, with a lighter complexion than Steve, but darker than Henry Berry. He has rather regular features, a high forehead and the brightest eyes of the three outlaws I met. He has a short, black beard, and straight, black hair, and is more refined in his appearance than Steve or Andrew Strong. He was armed precisely as they, with a rifle and two shotguns and a belt full of revolvers. He said he had heard of my presence in the neighborhood and was glad to see me.

It being now about one o'clock we were all naturally hungry, so Steve bought a couple dozen of eggs from a woman near by, who boiled them for him, and we went into the store at Moss Neck to eat them, which work we accomplished by cutting them in halves with our knives, sprinkling coarse salt on them and gulping down each half from its shell. I ate four, the remainder being devoured by the three outlaws. In addition to the eggs we had some

GINGER CAKE, CHEESE AND WRETCHED WHISKEY.

After dinner I was taken to McNeill's mill, near Moss Neck, the place where that Make (Malcolm) Sanderson was killed, and where, within a few yards of the former, one of his murderers, John Taylor, was subsequently punished. The place was pointed out to me, and the story of their respective deaths told by Andrew Strong.

WHERE MAKE SANDERSON AND JOHN TAYLOR WERE KILLED.

In September, 1870, Andrew, who up to that time had been charged with no offence, and was then working at his home, was called up from his bed at about eleven in the night by a party of over twenty men, who said they wanted him to go along with them a little ways. When he had dressed and gone out to the party he found they had another man (Make Sanderson) with them. After they had gone about a mile one of the party, McNeill, turned to Andrew and said, "You'll never see morning again," and upon his prisoner asking why and what he had done was answered that he was a d—d nigger and a spy for the Lowerys and so was Sanderson, and they had determined to kill them all.

On the road to Moss Neck they were shot by John Taylor, to whom the prisoners made a strong and passionate appeal for mercy, to which he replied, "If all the mulatto blood in the country was in you two and a movement of my foot would send you to hell I would make it." Soon after the prisoners were tied together and led to a secluded spot about a mile from Moss Neck, where they were to die. Sanderson asked for time to pray, which, after some consultation, was given him. In the midst of his supplications for pardon he was interrupted by a blow from a pistol and told to hurry up and not to pray so loud, as

GOD WOULD HEAR HIM ANYHOW.

When he had finished they were taken to a proper distance from their captors to be shot at, when Andrew, who had been working at his bonds ever since they were put on him, broke them suddenly and rushed for the woods, followed by the shots of his enemies.

Make Sanderson's body was found the next morning near McNeill's millpond riddled with bullets. It was said he was standing on a plank over the race, and at the first fire fell into the water still alive, and crawling out on the land below was shot on the ground where his mangled body was found.

For this murder John Taylor was arrested, but held to bail in the sum of $500. When H. B. Lowery heard this he remarked:

"We mulattoes must carry out our own laws: I will kill John Taylor," and on the morning of January 14, 1871, with a company of soldiers within 200 yards of him, he and Boss Strong rose from the road, a hundred yards from where Sanderson had been killed the fall before, and at a distance of less then ten yards shot the top of his head off.

AN OUTLAW CONCERT.

After Andrew had told me this history and had shown me where Sanderson and Taylor were killed, and where Henry and Boss were ambushed, we returned to the store, where for a couple of hours in a back room Steve and Andrew "picked" the banjo, played on the violin and sang negro melodies to an appreciative and enthusiastic audience. Steve sings very well, and the peculiar airs with which he was accompanied on the banjo were novel and exceedingly pleasant.

A LODGING PAID FOR.

When we finally left Moss Neck it was for the purpose of finding a place for me to spend the night. About three miles up the railroad we came to the residence of Tom Chavis to well-to-do mulatto, where Steve engaged lodging for me, telling them to give me a good supper and allow me to retire to bed immediately after, for I was "clean done worried out," and he would pay the bill; and, fixing a point to meet me the next day, the outlaws strode away toward the swamps.

THE PRESS ON THE OUTLAWS AND HERALD ENTERPRISE.

Our rural friends the Southern editors, are at it again. Past all their comprehension seems the fact that a New York journal could have a correspondent in Africa and one among the Carolina outlaws of the same time. Here, for instance, is an enlightened little rag from Mississippi, the *Pilot*. Hear what it flutters. Lord help a country with such pilots, although they do boast of being "official journal of the United States."

THROUGH THICK AND THIN.

(F m the Daily Mississippi Pilot, March 22).

One of the NEW YORK HERALD correspondents was recently killed while searching for Dr. Livingstone, in the interior of Africa, and now another has fallen into the hands of the Swamp Angels, led by the bandit, Stephen Lowery, in North Carolina. The Lowerys say they will not kill him; only interview him until they prove whether he is an impostor or not. Can't the HERALD spread this on a little thicker? It seems to us remarkably "thin."

THE HATE OF COLOR.

When the bull-fighters of Seville wish to enrage the plunging *toro* they flash a piece of red cloth before his eyes, and straightway he becomes mad. When you wish to enrage a grand old unprogressive, hardshell democrat of the Southern stripe show him something black, and the rabies will follow directly after. The following is the painful result of a Newark man finding out that the Lowerys were colored!

IF THEY WERE ONLY WHI

(From the Newark (N. J.,) Daily Journal, March 25.)

The Swamp Angels are not yet extinguished, and it is even a matter of doubt to the present time whether the leader is dead or has run away or will yet turn up in some fresh raid upon society. Would it not be well for Grant to extend a "protectorate" over Robeson county? The HERALD reporter has not yet been heard from, and when a whiteman, in the legitimate pursuit of an honorable busines, cannot pass safely through our own country, we think it would be better to postpone a protectorate over Mexico until we have regulated matters somewhat better at home. Had Henry Berry Lowery, and his gang been white men would they have been permitted to exist? We pause for a reply.

Here now is a southern man, who attends to his business of news collecting. We like this. He reports that the HERALD correspondent was in danger, and we are thankful to him:—

BRAVE RHODY LOWERY.

(From the Wilmington (N. C.) Journal, March 24.)

The wife of Henry Berry Lowery, the outlaw chief, was at Moss Neck depot yesterday as the train passed that point, whither she came for the purpose of delivering a despatch from Henderson, to be sent north from this city. She states that the correspondent was at Lowery's cabin, near Moss Neck, on Friday evening, about six o'clock, when Tom Lowery, Stephen Lowery, and Andrew Strong entered it and roughly told him to get up and go with them. He told them that he was ready; but first asked permission to send off a despatch to his paper, which was accorded him, when he wrote the despatch and gave it to the Lowery female, who, as we have seen, fulfilled her promise to deliver it to the conductor of the train. Henderson then accompanied the outlaws, bound for the recesses of Scuffletown swamp.

It was reported here yesterday, the report coming from Shoe Heel, that Henderson had been killed by the outlaws, but the report is generally discredited.

WHO IS TO BLAME?

Here is another solution of the question. The Edgefield *Advertiser* said it was Grant; the Raleigh *Era* said it was the Ku Klux; the Wilmington *Star* now says it is Governor Caldwell. Wonderful! It admits that he sent down his Adjutant General, but forgets to mention that the cowardice of the population of Robeson county made his efforts ineffectual. They can only tell half truths down there.

(From the Wilmington Star, March 24.)

CALDWELL AND LOWERY

That Henry Berry Lowery and his little band of robbers and cutthroats should, for so long a time, set law and civilization at defiance—should pillage, outrage and murder with un paralleled impunity—affords food for reflection upon the sort of government we have, and more especially gives ample opportunity to know the men who pretend to administer that government in the interest of justice, of law, of humanity.

It is a melancholy thought that is forced upon the intelligent North Carolinian, that the government of his native State is inadequate to protect him from the ravages of the highway robber and the bullet of the midnight assassin.

Low, indeed, is the condition of that people who are in daily jeopardy of life and property. Terrible is the state of that society that must thus live in constant peril.

We charge it upon Governer Caldwell—and his conduct sustains the charge—that he has been lax, lukewarm and careless in this matter of putting down the Lowerys.

We charge it upon him, that while innocent blood of good men appeared to him from the swamps and plains of Robeson and invoked high heaven for vengeance, he lifted scarce a little finger to arrest the dangerous course of the assassins, was dumb to piteous entreaty, heeded not the cries of consternation that went up to Him from a suffering, outraged, imperilled people.

We charge these things home upon the Governor of North Carolina, and the people know that the facts sustain the charge.

He was appealed to for a long while in vain.

He was appealed to persistently, and after taking much time he sent his Adjutant General to the scene on the outrages.

The result was a failure.

When he should have renewed again and again his exertions to capture or kill the outlaws he refused altogether to act.

But to-day, in North Carolina, not a hundred miles from Wilmington, we have a band of men, not a half dozen in number, who are open and notorious desperadoes, killing whom they list without the fear of punishment before their eyes, going at the dead hour of the night into towns, capturing iron safes and robbing them of their contents—a mere handful of men, riding roughshod over county, State and federal authorities, with a nonchalance and bravado that would do credit to the daring and subtle Bedouin of the desert.

Here, in the latter part of the nineteenth century, in a land that boasts of the excellency of its laws and the security afforded by its government, what do we see?

Alas! it would be well to be blind, if blindness brought contentment. But free citizens, with souls in their bodies, cannot shut their eyes to the attrocious violations of law, peace and order in Robeson county.

Men, with the common feelings of humanity—individuals upon whom one ray of the sun of civilization has shone—must experience pity, shame, and indignation at the spectacle of a petty gang of mulattoes committing act after act of the most fiendish outrage of law, deed after deed of the most abandoned savagery, perilling the industrial interests of a whole section, filling the public mind with apprehension and terror, and doing these diabolical crimes with almost the certainty of non-interference, if not protection, by a radical administration.

Upon the head of Tod R. Caldwell rests the responsibility, the terrible responsibility of the deeds of these murderous villains. Let him, and him alone, bear the blame and reap the deep curses of an outraged, afflicted people!

It will not do for his partisans to say that he could not suppress these pitiful outlaws. He did not try to put them down. He would have shown his humanity and his efficiency as a Governor had this band been composed of white men and his party had chosen to dub them Ku Klux. Oh, yes! What calling out of militia *a la* Holden! What making of requisitions upon Grant! What an upstir of loyalty! What an outburst of patriotic zeal would there have been had Lowery been a Ku Klux! Pity! pity! So much party capital is lost! Long ago would the little band have gone to the criminal's bourne, and the very name of Lowery have been a stench in loyal Northern nostrils, and a new hate of the South been added to the catalogue now long as the list of ships in Homer.

Again we pile up the counts in our bill of indictment. We charge it upon Governor Caldwell that he can meddle in law-making, can make himself Legislature and Supreme Court, can starve Penitentiary convicts and drive inmates of the Asylums from the place of medical aid back to their homes. We charge it upon Governor Caldwell that he is forward and meddlesome and obstinate and cruel where these virtuous and praiseworthy quualities of his head and heart can be bestowed upon conservative enemies. We charge it upon Governor Caldwell that he so despises our party that he cannot in his official conduct do members of that party any justice.

Governor Caldwell that he does not make a hearty and an earnest effort to stop the reign of lawlessness, rapine and murder around Scuffletown and Moss Neck. We charge it upon Governor Caldwell that he is callous and brutally indifferent to the higher instincts of humanity, that he is active only in belief of party, zealous only when party exigency requires zeal; that he would long since have stopped the Robeson outrages if the Outlaws had been conservative whites instead of radical blacks. These charges are preferred by the whole body of intelligent, law-abiding people of the State whom he disgraces and outrages. If he quails not before them, if their indignant voices move not his rough, fretful, splenetic and savage nature, then is he sunk and sodden in the lowest pit of degradation, and there is no hope for him, then is he forever damned in the estimation of all good and peaceable citizens.

THE END.

[NOTE.—Many of the foregoing articles are introduced merely to explain how such a state of things could possibly exist in a civilized country. The fierce hate of political factionists entirely blinding them to the disgrace and injury inflicted upon their common country by the toleration of wrong deeds whether perpetrated by one class or another.]

www.ingramcontent.com/pod-product-compliance
Lightning Source LLC
Chambersburg PA
CBHW022144090426
42742CB00010B/1378